SCOTLAND

A-Z Visitors' Atlas & Guide

KU-361-259

CONTENTS

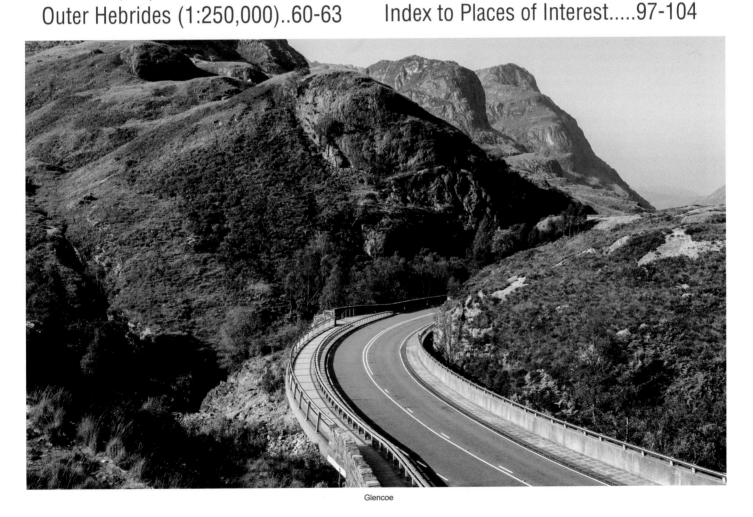

Glencoe

EDITION 7 2018
Copyright © Geographers' A-Z Map Company Ltd.

registered trade marks of
Geographers' A-Z Map Company Ltd

Motorway	M8
Motorway Under Construction	
Motorway Proposed	
Motorway Junctions with Numbers	
Unlimited Interchange	4
Limited Interchange	5
Motorway Service Area	S
with access from one carriageway only	S
Major Road Service Area (with 24 hour facilities)	
Primary Route	S
Class A Road	S
Major Road Junctions	
Detailed / Other	4
Primary Route	A92
Primary Route Junction with Number	5
Primary Route Destination	OBAN

Dual Carriageways (A & B roads)	
Class A Road	A814
Class B Road	B9080
Narrow Major Road (passing places)	
Major Roads Under Construction	
Major Roads Proposed	
Safety Cameras with Speed Limits	
Single Camera	30
Multiple Cameras located along road	50
Single & Multiple Variable Cameras	V V
Fuel Station	
Gradient 1:7 (14%) & steeper	≫ ≫
Toll	Toll
Remote Payment System	
Park & Ride	P+R
Mileage between markers	8
Airport	✈
Airfield	+
Heliport	H

Ferry	
(vehicular, sea)	
(vehicular, river)	
(foot only)	
Railway and Station	
Level Crossing and Tunnel	
River or Canal	
County or Unitary Authority Boundary	
National Boundary	
Built-up Area	
Town, Village or Hamlet	
Wooded Area	
Spot Height in Feet	813 ·
Relief above 400' (122m)	
National Grid Reference (kilometres)	8 00
Page Continuation	48
Area covered by Town Plan	SEE PAGE 84

Queensferry Crossing

reproduced courtesy of Transport Scotland

TOURIST INFORMATION

Abbey, Church, Friary, Priory	†
Animal Collection	
Aquarium	
Arboretum, Botanical Garden	
Aviary, Bird Garden	
Battle Site and Date	1066
Blue Flag Beach	
Bridge	
Butterfly Farm	
Castle (open to public)	
Castle with Garden (open to public)	
Cathedral	✝
Cidermaker	
Country Park	
Distillery	
Farm Park, Open Farm	

Fortress, Hill Fort	
Garden (open to public)	
Golf Course	
Historic Building (open to public)	
Historic Building with Garden (open to public)	
Horse Racecourse	
Industrial Monument	
Leisure Park, Leisure Pool	
Lighthouse	
Mine, Cave	
Monument	
Motor Racing Circuit	
Museum, Art Gallery	M
National Park	
National Trust Property	

Natural Attraction	★
Nature Reserve or Bird Sanctuary	
Nature Trail or Forest Walk	
Picnic Site	
Place of Interest	Craft Centre ·
Prehistoric Monument	
Railway, Steam or Narrow Gauge	
Roman Remains	
Theme Park	
Tourist Information Centre	i
Viewpoint (360 degrees) / (180 degrees)	
Vineyard	
Visitor Information Centre	V
Wildlife Park	
Windmill	
Zoo or Safari Park	

SCALE

1:200,000   3.156 miles to 1 inch (2.54 cm) / 2 km (1.243 miles) to 1 cm

| 0 | 1 | 2 | 3 | 4 | 5 | | 10 | | 15 | | 20 miles |

| 0 | 1 | 2 | 3 | 4 | 5 | | 10 | 15 | 20 | 25 | 30 kilometres |

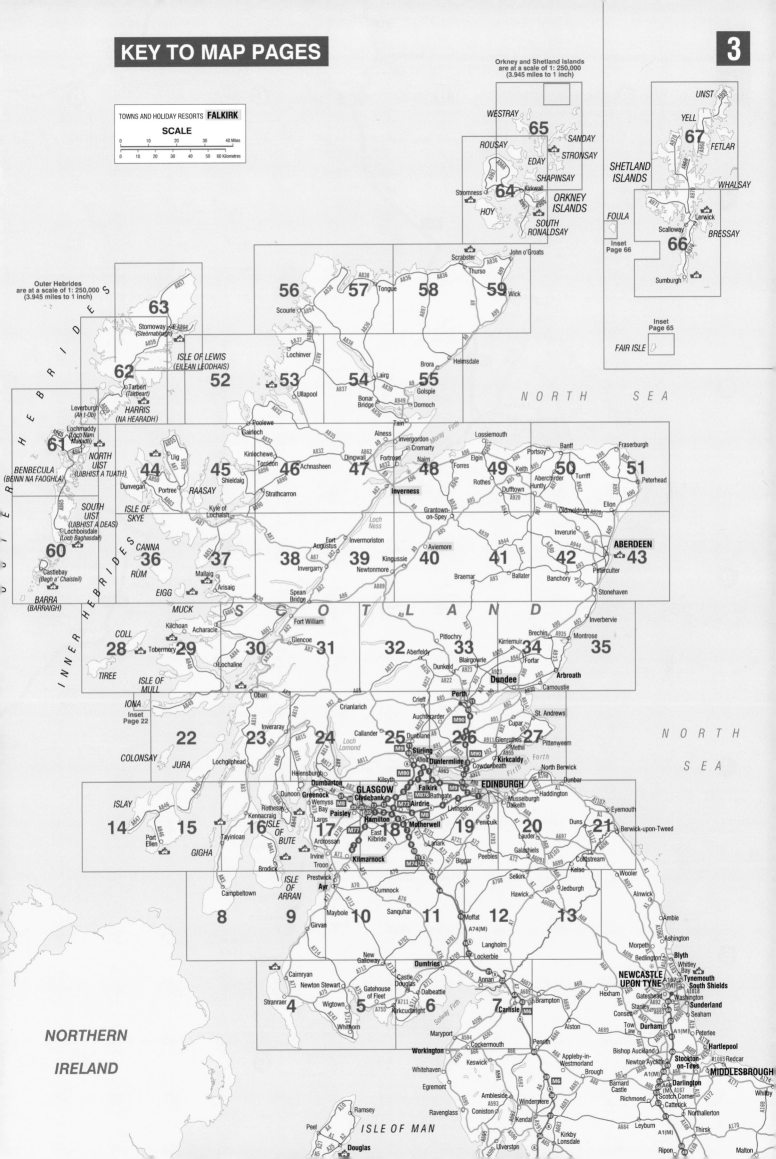

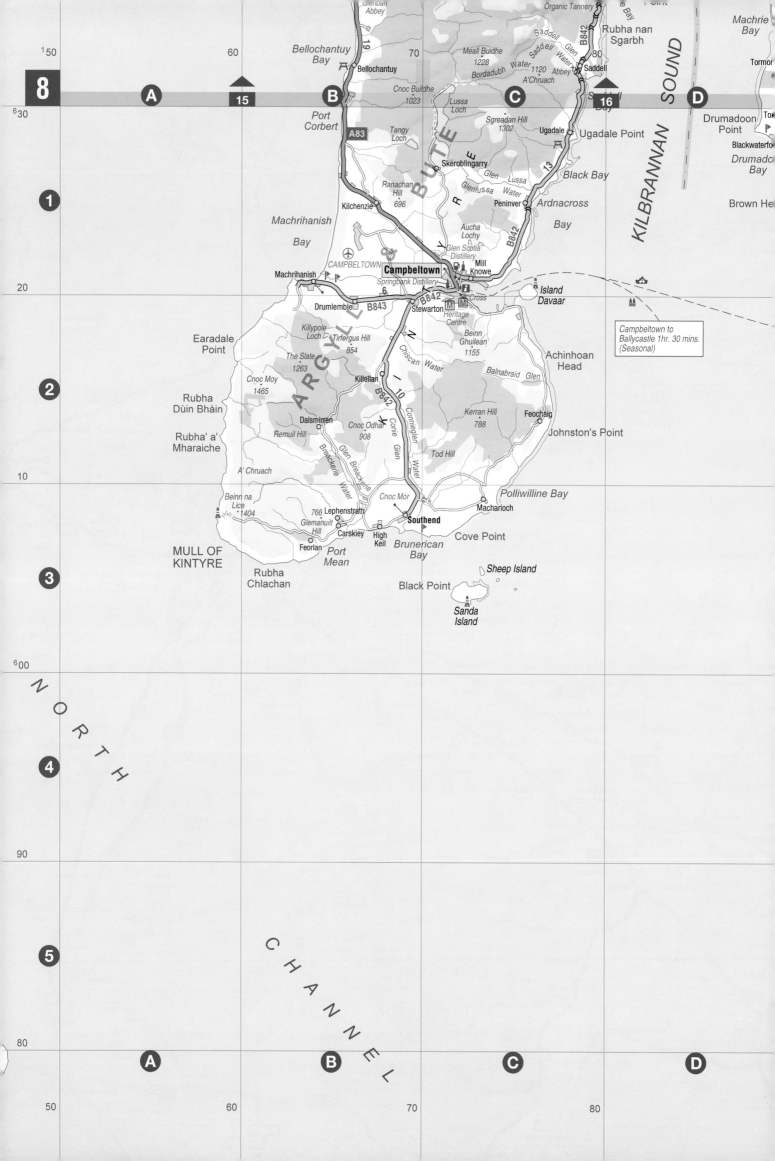

Nave Isla

Eilean
Beag

Ardnave
Loch

Tòn Mhór

Loch
Laingeadàil   Kilnave

Loch Còrr   Sanaigmore   Loch an
Fhir Mhór

Braigo

Rubha
Lamanais   Grulinbeg

Leckgruinart

Gr

B8017

Saligo Bay

Loch Gorm

S

Saligo

Coul
Point   I Castle   B8018

Distillery   7   A8

Machir
Bay   Kilchoman   ISLAY   Conisby   Carrai
Dhub

Cnoc Dubh   Distillery   Bruichladdich

Kilchiaran   Kilchiaran

Kilchiaran
Bay   Loch
Gearach   Islay
Life   Natural History
Centre

Octomore   M   Port
Charlotte

Cultoon
Stone Circle   Beinn Tart
a' Mhill
760

Lossit   Laggan

Lossit
Bay   Neribus   Laggan
Point

Octofad

RHINNS   Port Gleann
na Gaoidh   Lag

Portnahaven   A847

Orsay   Port Wemyss   B

RHINNS POINT

Slugaide
Glas

Glena
Loc

Dùn Mór Ghil   T

Lower
Killeyan   American
Monument
MULL OF OA   Beinn
66

Oban to Lochboisdale 5hrs. 20m (Seasonal)

Oban to Castlebay 5hrs.

Cairns of
Eag na
Maoile
Rubha Mór
Eilean
Bousd
Cornaigmore
Sorisdale
Rubh'a' Bhinnein
COLL
Loch
Fada
Cliad Bay
Bagh Feisdlum
Grishipoll
Rubha Hogh
Clabhach
B8011
Loch Cliad
Hogh Bay
340
Ben Nogh
Loch nan
Arinagour
Stables
Cinneachan
V
Loch
Totronald
Anlaimh
Loch Eathana
Feall
Coll
Acha
Eilean
Bay
Uig
5
Ornsay
Calgary Point
Friesland
Port na
h-Eathar
Gunna
Caolas Bàn
Bay
Oban to Tiree 3hrs. 20mins. (Seasonal)
Crossapol
Bay
Port
Soa
Coll to Tiree 55mins.
Rubha Dubh
a' Mhurain
HEBRIDES

Tiree to Barra 2hrs. 45mins. (Seasonal)

Hough
Skerries
Vaul
Miodar
Bay
Carnan
Balephetrish
Sraid
Cornaigmore
Bay
Vaul
Salum
5
Ruadh
Balephetrish
Loch
Caolas
Balevullin
Riaghain
B8069
Kilmoluaig
Cornaigbeg
Gott
Ruaig
Hough
5
Kenovay
Kirkapol
Isles
Kilkenneth
TIREE
Gott Bay
(Port Adhair Thiriodh)
Sandaig
An
Moss
Iodhlann
Middleton
B8065
Baugh
Scarinish
Port Mor
2
Barrapol
Crossapol
Héanish
Rubha Tràigh
Port
Island Life
Heylipol
an Duin
Bharrapool
Loch a'
4
Phuill
Hynish
TIREE
Balephuil
3
Bay
Balemartine
B8067
Mannal
Treshnish
Lunga
Balephuil
B8068
West
Bay
Hynish
Hynish
Bac Mor or
Port Snoig
Skerryvore
Dutchman's Cap
Lighthouse
Bac Beag

INNER

Réidh
Eilean
Eilean
Annraic

IONA

MUCK

Eilean nan Each
Gòdag
Port Mor
Dubh Sgeir

Sound of Eigg

An Sgurr 1292
Sandavore
Sgeir Eskernish
Galmisdale
Eilean Chathastail

Mallaig to Muck 35mins. (Seasonal)
Eigg to Muck 35mins.
1hr. 40mins. (Mins.)

Land, Sea and Islands Centre
Glen Cottage
Druimindarroch
Prince's Cairn

Rubh Arisaig
Eilean a' Ghaill
Eilean an t-Snidhe

Sound of Arisaig
Eilean nan Gobhar

Samalaman Island
Glenuig Bay
Roshven
A861

Samalaman
Glenuig (Gleann Uige)
Smirisary
Loch na Cloiche Sgoilte
Lochan na Cloiche Sgoilte

Coll to Oban 2hrs. 45mins.

ARDNAMURCHAN

Sanna Point
Sanna Bay
Sanna
Achnaha
Portuairk
Ardnamurchan Lighthouse
Point of Ardnamurchan
Achosnich

Fascadale
Achateny
Kilmory
Branault
Ockle Point
Ockle
Port Bàn

Rubh' Aird an Fheidh
Rubha Aird Druimnich
Eilean Shona
Baramore
Arean
Farquhar's Point
Ardtoe
Newton of Ardtoe
Gortenfern
Gortenorn
Kentra Bay
Kentra
Arivegaig
Shielfoot
Blain
Langal
Dalnabreck
Mingarrypark
Moss
Ardshealach
Acharacle (Ath-Tharracail)

Loch Moidart
Castle Tioram
Kinlochmoidart (Ceann Loch Muideirt)
Ardmolich
Brune
Dal
A861

Meall nan Con 1433

B8007
Loch Mudle
Beinn nan Losgann 1026

Loch Laga
Meall nan Each 1607
Leac Shoilleir
Lochan nam Fiann
Loch Sligneach
Ben Laga 1679
A861
Salen (An Sailean)
Resipole

Beinn Bhraec 1171

B8044

Kilchoan
Ormsaigmore
Ormsaigbeg
Mingary
Mingary Castle
Kilchoan Bay
An-Acairseid

Ben Hiant 1731
Cladh Chiaran Burial Ground
Glenmore
Glenbeg
Ardnamurchan Natural History Centre
Glenborrodale
Laga
B8007
Ardslignish
Maclean's Nose
35mins.

Oronsay
Risga
Carna
Glencripesdale Burn
Meall an Damhain 1693
30

HIGHLAND

Beinn Iadain 1873

Kinloch

Lochanan Dubha

MORVERN

Beinn na h-Uamha
Claggan
A884
10
50

Quinish Point
Glengorm Castle
Croig
Calgary
Calgary Bay
Caliach Point

Ardmore Bay
Ardmore Point
Rubha nan Gall
An Tobar
Meall an Inbhire 865
An Mull
Isle of Mull Cheese
M
Tobermory
Hebridean Whale and Dolphin Trust
V
Tobermory Distillery
Calve Island

Auliston Point

Drimnin

Beinn Bhuidhe 1481
1806
Sithean na Raplaich
An t-Aoineadh Mor Deserted Village
Loch Arienas

B849
Rhemore
Killundine
Caisteal nan Con
Fiunary
Fiunary Forest
Larachbeg
Ardtornish
Achranich Rannoch
A884
Lochaline
Glais Bheinn 1570

eshnish Point
Ensay
Haunn
Burg
Kilninian
Achleck
Fanmore
Ballygown

Dervaig
B8073
'S Airde Beinn 959
Loch an Torr
Loch Peallach
Cruachan Druim na Croise 866
Loch Frisa
Speinne Mór 1458
Lettermore
Ardnacross
A848
Tenga
Aros

AROS

Sound of Mull

Aros Mains
Aros Castle
Rubha Mór
Salen
13
A849
Fishnish Bay
Fishnish
Bailemeonach
Garmony
Ardtornish Castle
Inninmore Bay
40

Rubh a' Chaoil
Eilean Dioghlum
Gometra House
Gometra

ULVA

Loch Tuath
Cnoc an da Chinn 1280
Beinn na Drise 1392
Eas Fors Waterfall
Laganulva
Oskamull
Isle of Ulva Heritage Centre
Ulva House
B8073
Kellan
Killiechronan
Gruline
B8035
Knock
Loch na Keal
Loch na Dairidh
Macquarie Mausoleum
Beinn Bhuidhe 1352
Beinn Chreagach Mhór 1903
Scallastle Bay
Craignure Bay
Craignure

Mâisgeir
Eilean na Creiche
Samalan Island
Inch Kenneth
B8035
Eorsa
Derryguaig
Gribun
Beinn a' Ghràig 1939
Tomsléibhe
Dùn da Ghaoithe 2512
Oakbank
A849
30

Staffa
Fingal's Cave
Little Colonsay
Erisgeir

BEN MORE 3171
Coirc Bheinn 1837
Corra-bheinn 2311
Beinn Talaidh 2502
Sgurr Dearg 2429
Loch an Doire Dharaich
Lochan an Doire Dharaich
Loch Bearnach
A849

ISLE OF MULL

Glen Cannel
Glen More
Lussa River
Strathcoil
Loch Sguabain
Loch Airdeglais
Carn Ban 812

ARDMEANACH
Rubha na h Uamha 1613
Creach Bheinn
MacCulloch's Fossil Tree
Tavool House
Tiroran
Port na Croise
Kilfinichen Bay
B8035
22
Scridain
Pennyghael
Beinn na Croise 1649
A849
Lochbuie
Ben Buie 2354
Creach Beinn 2290
Kinlochspelve
Loch Spelve
Croggan
Moy Castle
Standing Stone Circle
Loch Uisg

rubha Cearc
Kintra
Creich
Garbh Phort
Torrans
Ardtun
Bun an
Leidle
Ardbrishnish

Leachie Hill

Brae of Glenbervie

Tolbooth

Castle Haven

Dunnottar

...tochty Forest

Glenfarquhar Lodge

Bervie Water

Burnes Memorial

A90

A92

Thornyhive Bay

80

Finalla

Herscha Hill 723

Glenbervie

Drumlith...

42

Bruxie Hill 711

Crawton

Auchenblae

...rest

Bridge of Mondynes

Milton of Barras

Roadside of Catterline

Crawton Bay

B966

Fordoun

Parkneuk

Catterline

Braidon Bay

HIRE

17

Grassic Gibbon Centre

Roadside of Kinneff

Fernieflatt

Todhead Point

MEARNS

Bridge of Kair

Arbuthnott House

Arbuthnott

B967

Kinneff

Little John's Haven

...ncekirk

Easter Tulloch

Knox Hill

Inverbervie

Bervie Bay

...est ...side

Garvock

Maggie Law Lifeboat

Gourdon

50

Benholm

Mill

B9120

Chapelfield

A92

Johnshaven

Lochside

13

St Cyrus

...gie Pathhead

Air Station

William Lamb Sculpture Studio

MONTROSE

NORTH

Ferryden

...rkton Craig.

Usan

SEA

...nald

Boddin Point

Lunan

Bay

Red Head

Bell Rock 80

Port Erroll
Chapel Hill
Bogbrae Croft
Bay of Cruden

bank
Inverebrie
Yonderton
Broomfield
Ellon
arrachie
Esslemont Castle
Denhead
Meikle Loch
Whinnyfold

Castle
Kirkton of Logie Buchan
Collieston
B9003
Old Slains Castle
Kirktown of Slains

Tipperty
Meikle Tarty
Forvie
Knockhall Castle

Hill of Fiddes

Newburgh
Hackley Head or Forvie Ness

Foveran
Newburgh Bar

Tillery
Drums

Craigie

Whitecairns

Balmedie

Belhelvie

Potterton
DANGER AREA

Blackdog

Corby Loch

Bridge of Don

Aberdeen to:
Kirkwall (Hatston) 6hrs.
Lerwick (Holmsgarth)
12hrs. 30mins.

Zoology

Hayton

Cruickshank Botanic
Old Aberdeen

Kittybrewster

Kings Museum

ABERDEEN SEE PAGE 69

Footdee
Maritime
Torry

Nigg Bay

ofield

Ferryhill

David Welch Winter

Kincorth

Nigg
Doonies Farm

rleston

nchory
evenick

Charlestown

Cove Bay
Souter Head

Portlethen
Hillside
Findon

Portlethen Village

Cammachmore Bay
Downies

Cammachmore

Newtonhill

halls

onie Point

Point

N O R T H   S E A

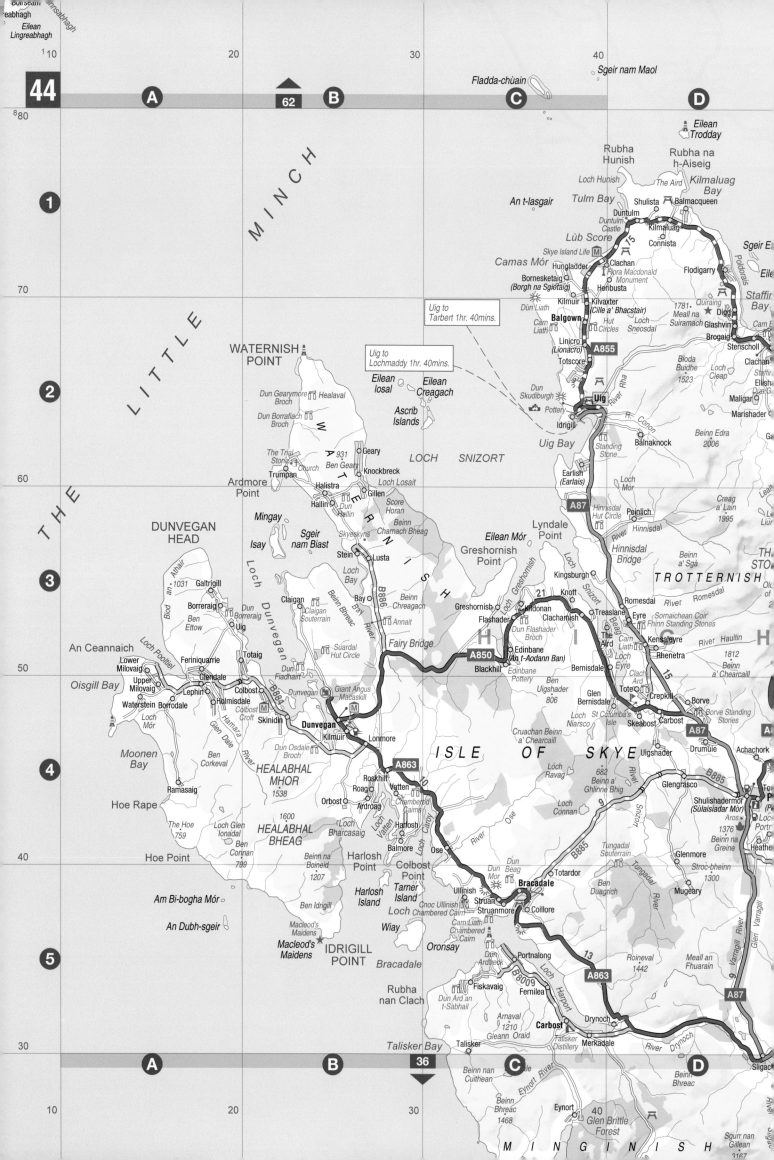

E   F   G   H

4 00   10   20   30

80

1

70

N O R T H   S E A

2

60

3

50

4

40

5

E   F   43   G   H

8 30

10   20   4 30

Kinnaird Head
Scottish Lighthouses
Heritage Centre
sehearty   B9031   Pittulie   Broadsea
Sandhaven
Pitsligo Castle
Peathill
Percyhorner
Kirktown
Fraserburgh
Fraserburgh Bay
Cairnbulg Point
Cairnbulg
Maggie's Hoosie
Inverallochy
Charlestown
St Combs
Inzie Head
A98
A981
A90
B9033
B910
Cairnbulg Castle
Moss-side of Cairness
Gowanhill
Inverallochy Castle
Mid Ardlaw
Cardno
Memsie
Rathen
Cairness
Blackhills
Corsehill
Hillhead of Auchentumb
Memsie Cairn
Crimonmogate
Loch of Strathbeg
Rattray Head
Middlemuir
Waughton Hill
768
White Horse
White Stag
Dartfield
Crimond
Rattray
A952
Cockmuir
Belfatton
Longhill
Keyhead
Strichen
New Leeds
Rowanhill
Balearn
St Fergus Moss
Middle Essie
Shielhill
Gallowhills
Kirktown
St Fergus
Adziel
North Ugie
Denhead
Hythie
Backfolds
Rora Moss
Cuttyhill
Rora
A981
B9093
B9093
Forest of Deer
Fetterangus
Drinnie's Wood Observatory
Dunshillock
Ravenscraig Castle
River Ugie
Inverugie
Brucklay
C H A N
Owl & ssycat entre
Loudon Wood Stone Circle
Maud
Old Deer
Mintlaw
Longside
Buchanhaven
Peterhead
B9029
Deer Abbey
Aden
Aberdeenshire Farming
South Ugie Water
Flushing
Arbuthnot
A950
Keith Inch
Backhill of Clackriach
Quartalehouse
Stuartfield
Inverquhomery
Peterhead
A982
Burnhaven
Invernettie
Bulwark
Millbreck
Little Dens
Cocklaw
Drymuir
B9030
Kinnadie
Clola
Boddam
Stirling
Boddam Castle
chnagatt
Mains of Auchnagatt
Nether Kinmundy
Blackhill
Sandfordhill
A90
Kinknockie
Coldwells
Long Haven
Milton Coldwells
A952
Muirtack
Hill of Dudwick
570
Hatton
Bullers of Buchan
North Haven
A975
Twa Havens
ide
uox
Arthrath
Bridgend
Cruden Bay
Slains Castle
Port Erroll
Chapel Hill
whindle
A948
Bogbrae Croft
Bay of Cruden
bank
Inverebrie
Yonderton
Broomfield
Whinnyfold
harrachie
Elton
Castle
Denhead
Meikle Loch
Old Slains Castle
Esslemont Castle
P+R
A90
B9003
Kirkton of Slains
A920
E
B9005
Kirkton of Logie Buchan
Collieston
A975
Tipperty
Meikle
Forvie
Hackley Head or Forvie Ness
Knockhall Castle
B9000
B9000
Hill of Fiddes
Newburgh

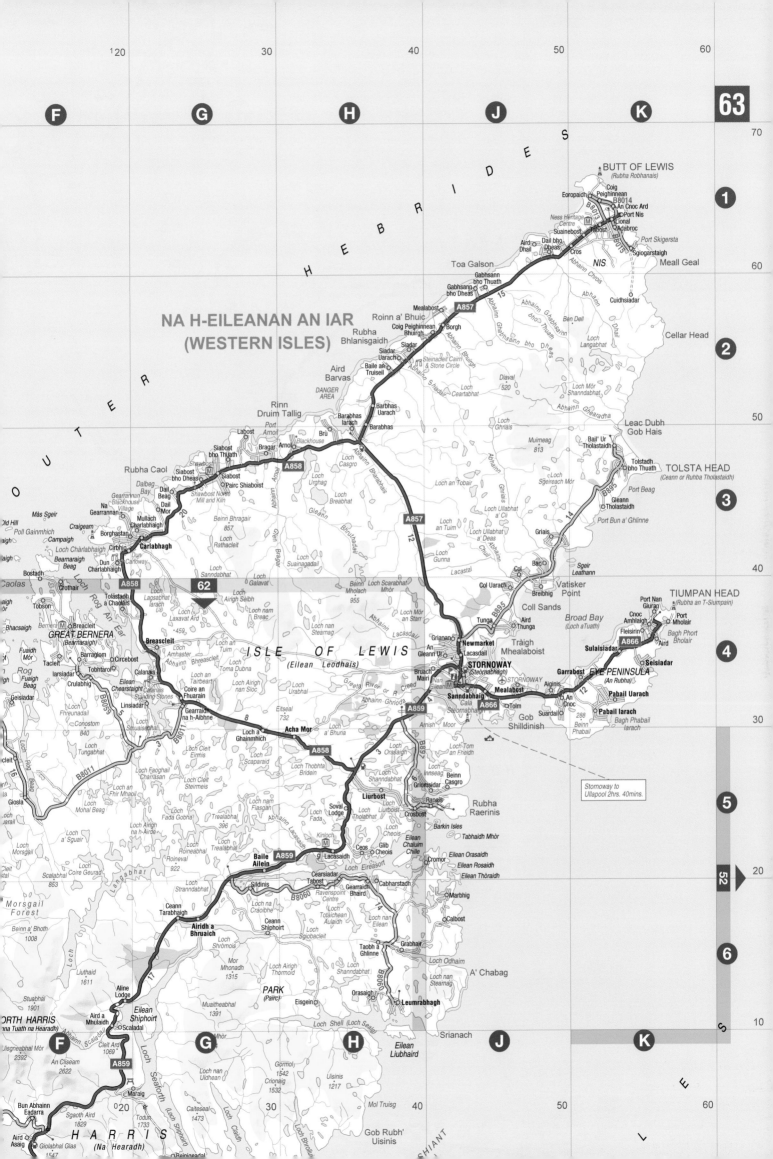

ORKNEY ISLANDS

Fair Isle lies about 27 miles ENE of North Ronaldsay

Fair Isle to Grutness / Sumburgh 2hrs. 30mins

Fair Isle to Lerwick 5hrs. (Seasonal)

Skroo

North Haven

FAIR ISLE

Stonybreck

Leogh

Fair Isle

South Harbour

SHETLAND ISLANDS

Westray / Papa Westray area
The Bore
Mull Head
Papa Westray
PAPA WESTRAY
Holm of Papa
Knap of Howar
Holm of Papa Westray Chambered Cairn
Holland
Bay of Skail
Backaskaill
Loch of St Tredwell
Noup Head
Bay of Noup
Rack Wick
Rackwick
Gayfield
Monivey
Nottland
Pierowall
20mins. (Seasonal)
Papa Westray to North Ronaldsay 1hr. 10mins. (Seasonal)
Westray Heritage Centre
Broughton
Braehead
Bay of Cleat
WESTRAY
Cleat
Bay of Swanmill
THE NORTH SOUND
B9067
Skel Wick
Fitty Hill 555
Midbea
8
Skelwick
B9066
Westside Church
Bay of Tuquoy
Rack Wick
Rapness
Skea Skerries
40mins.

North Ronaldsay
Garso Wick
Seal Skerry
North Ronaldsay
NORTH RONALDSAY
Linklet Bay
Hollandstoun
South Bay

NORTH RONALDSAY FIRTH
Holmes of Ire
Whitemill Bay
North Loch
Roos Wick
Scar
Bay of Sandquoy
Northwall
Lettan
Scuthvie Bay
Burness
Otters Wick
B9069
Newark
Start Point
North Bay
Bay of Lopeness
Bay of Brough
SANDAY
Broughtown
Lady
SANDAY
B9068
Overbister
Bay of Newark
Kettletoft
Kettletoft Bay
Backaskaill Bay
Sty Wick
Quoyness Chambered Cairn
Tres Ness
Kirkwall to North Ronaldsay 2hrs. 40mins.

64 / Westray Firth
WESTRAY FIRTH
Kirkwall to Westray 1hr. 25mins.
Wart Holm
Rusk Holm
Rapness Sound
Sound of Faray
Calf of Eday
Carrick Ho
Calfsound
Benstonhall
Faray
Mill Bay
Millbounds
Lamiless
Braeswick
Stove
Fersness Bay
Bay of London
B9063
5
Bay of Stove
Sanday Sound
EDAY
Bay of Backland
Backaland
The Keld
35mins. (Seasonal)
Southside
Veness
Spurness Sound
35mins.
Holm of Huip
Papa Stronsay
Kirkwall to Eday 1hr. 15mins.

Rousay / Egilsay / Wyre
Saviskaill Bay
B9064
Wasbister
Kierfea Hill 771
Midhowe Broch
Midhowe Chambered Cairn
ROUSAY
Muckle Water
Sourin
St Magnus Kirk
Kili Holm
St Magnus Kirk
Eynhallow
Westside
Church
Westness
Blotchnie Fold
Cairns 821
Brinian
Egilsay
B9064
7
Frotoft
Eynhallow Sound
Wyre Sound
Cubbie Roo's Castle
Wyre
St Mary's Chapel
Muckle Green Holm
Holm of Huip
Odie
STRONSAY
Whitehall
Linga
Linga Holm
Mill Bay
B9062
B9060
3
St Catherine's Bay
Linga Sound
Samsonslane
Everbay
STRONSAY
Bay of Bomasty
B9061
Grobister
Odin Bay
Kirbuster
Rothiesholm
Dishes
Cott
Bay of Holland
Holland
Bay of Houseby

Mainland / Kirkwall
B966
Eynhallow
Costa
Geargh
Stenso
Redland
B9057
Hillside
Woodwick
Tingwall
17
Click Mill
Wass Wick
A966
Milldoe 726
Hackland
Gorseness
Wood Wick
Gairsay Sound
Sweyn Holm
Mirbister
Corrigall Farm
Corrigall
Isbister
Gairsay
Settiscarth
Bay of Isbister
Burroughston
Brough
A986
Bay of Furrowend
Bimbister
Wide Firth
Veantrow Bay
Edmonstone
B9058
Bay of Linton
Grimeston
Finstown
Damsay
Bay of Firth
Thieves Holm
Crossgate
Balfour
SHAPINSAY
Cuween Hill Chambered Cairn
Rennibister Earth House
A965
Helliar Holm
B9059
Heddle
Grimbister
Grain Earth-house
Work
Newlot
Bay of Mel
Wideford Hill Chambered Cairn
Orkney Wireless
The String
Shapinsay Sound
Tormiston Mill
Keelylang Hill 721
M
Bishop's Palace
Kirkwall
Yinstay
Linksness
A965
Highland Park Distillery
KIRKWALL
Inganess Bay
Loch of Tankerness
M A I N L A N D
Scapa
Tradespark
A964
Greenigoe
Borrowstonehill
Scapa Bay
A961
Tankerness
Toab
Deer Sound
Den Wick
ORKNEY ISLANDS

Kirkwall (Hatston) to:
Aberdeen 7hrs. 15mins.
Lerwick (Holmsgarth) 7hrs. 45mins.

Kirkwall (Hatston) to:
Aberdeen 7hrs. 15mins.
Lerwick (Holmsgarth) 7hrs. 45mins.

Southern Mainland
Ward Hill 883
Kirbister
Loch of Kirbister
DANGER AREA
Hobbister
A964
Orphir Earl's Bu
Swanbister
Smoogro
Waulkmill Bay
Midland
Orphir Church
Swanbister Bay
B9052
Gritley
Deerness
Skaills
Sandside Bay
B9050
Graemeshall
Burn
Foubister
Upper Sanday
Newark Bay
Horse of Copinsay

STRONSAY FIRTH
Auskerry Sound
Ingale Skerry
Auskerry
Shapinsay Sound

B9064
B9057
A966
A986
A965
A964
A961
A960
B9050
B9051
B9052

TOWN PLAN PAGES

St Monans

REFERENCE

MOTORWAY	M8
MOTORWAY UNDER CONSTRUCTION	
MOTORWAY PROPOSED	
MOTORWAY JUNCTIONS WITH NUMBERS	4 5
Unlimited Interchange 4	
Limited Interchange 5	
PRIMARY ROUTE	A92
DUAL CARRIAGEWAYS	
CLASS A ROAD	A804
CLASS B ROAD	B700
MAJOR ROADS UNDER CONSTRUCTION	
MAJOR ROADS PROPOSED	
MINOR ROAD	
SAFETY CAMERA (with Speed Limits)	30
FUEL STATION	
RESTRICTED ACCESS	
PEDESTRIANIZED ROAD & MAIN FOOTWAY	
ONE-WAY STREET	
TOLL	TOLL
RAILWAY AND STATION	
LEVEL CROSSING AND TUNNEL	
BUILT-UP AREA	
ABBEY, CATHEDRAL, PRIORY ETC.	†

AIRPORT	✈
BUS STATION	
CAR PARK (Selection of)	P
CHURCH	†
CITY WALL	
FERRY (Vehicular)	
(Foot only)	
GOLF COURSE	
HELIPORT	
HOSPITAL	H
LIGHTHOUSE	
MARKET	
NATIONAL TRUST FOR SCOTLAND PROPERTY	
(Open) _ NTS (Restricted Opening) _ NTS	
PARK & RIDE	P+R
PLACE OF INTEREST	
POLICE STATION	▲
POST OFFICE	★
SHOPPING PRECINCT	
SHOPMOBILITY	
TOILET	▽
TOURIST INFORMATION CENTRE	i
VIEWPOINT	
VISITOR INFORMATION CENTRE	V

ABERDEEN

Aberdeen is the third largest city in Scotland, famed for its splendid granite architecture. A Royal Burgh since the 12th century, it is home to one of the oldest universities in Britain and it has an important maritime history and with the offshore North Sea oil industry it remains one of Britain's busiest harbours. To the north of the city is Old Aberdeen and though it has been incorporated with the main part of the city since 1891, it maintains its own ambience. Old Aberdeen is primarily associated with the university and the distinctive crown spire of Kings College, founded in 1495 by Bishop Elphinstone during the reign of King James IV. Later in 1860 King's college would combine with Marischal College in the main part of the city (see below) to form the University of Aberdeen. Today, most visitor attractions centre on the main part of the city along Union Street and its environs. From here it is a short walk to the harbour that has played a significant role in shaping Aberdeen's prosperity since the 12th century when shipping tithes were first introduced. Ferries to Orkney and the Shetlands leave from the quay and the fish market can be visited Monday to Friday. The Aberdeen International Youth Festival takes place each year usually at the beginning of August and attracts many young performers from around the world who descend on the city for ten days to showcase their talents. Aberdeen is a diverse city with a wide spectrum of attractions that make it an attractive tourist destination throughout the year.

PLACES OF INTEREST

Visit Scotland Information Centre (All Year) - 23 Union Street. AB11 5BP.
Tel: (01224) 269180

◆ ABERDEEN ART GALLERY - This popular attraction houses an important fine art collection with paintings, sculptures and graphics from the 15th to 21st century, a rich and diverse applied art collection, an exciting programme of special exhibitions. Gallery shop and café. Schoolhill.

◆ ABERDEEN ARTS CENTRE & THEATRE: ACT - community theatre and art gallery. 33 King Street.

◆ ABERDEEN CATHEDRAL - Perpendicular Gothic style episcopal church dating from 1817 and subsequently gaining Cathedral status in 1914. Within the cathedral is an exhibition that reflects the history of Christianity in the north east of Scotland. King Street.

◆ ABERDEEN MARITIME MUSEUM - The museum highlights the history of the North Sea using models, paintings and computer interactives. The offshore oil industry is brought to life using the world's largest oil platform model. This attraction includes one of Aberdeen's oldest buildings, Provost Ross's House, built in 1593. Shop, café. Shiprow.

◆ ABERDEEN MERCAT CROSS - Dating from 1686, Aberdeen's mercat cross is regarded as the finest example in Scotland. It depicts a unicorn mounted on a hexagonal base on which are panels with medallion heads of the ten Stuart monarchs together with heraldic coats-of-arms. Justice Street.

◆ ABERDEEN RC CATHEDRAL - Gothic revival Victorian cathedral dating from 1860-80. 20 Huntly Street.

◆ ABERDEEN TOLBOOTH MUSEUM - One of the city's oldest buildings, the Tolbooth was once a gaol. As a museum it describes the history of crime and punishment in Aberdeen. Visit the 17th & 18th Century cells with their original doors and barred windows. Interactive displays and exhibitions. Castle Street.

◆ KIRK OF ST NICHOLAS - Dating from the 12th century, this is the original parish church of Aberdeen. Only the transepts remain of the original structure and modifications have continued into the 20th century with the addition of Scottish stained glass. Back Wynd.

◆ MARISCHAL COLLEGE - Famed as the world's second largest granite structure. The present buildings date predominantly from the 19th century and the neo-Gothic west front is regarded as one of the world's finest architectural achievements in granite. Broad Street. (Currently occupied by Aberdeen City Council).

◆ PEACOCK VISUAL ARTS - Contemporary art exhibitions and events. Digital, photography and printmaking workshops. 21 Castle Street.

◆ PROVOST SKENE'S HOUSE - This 16th century house captures the grandeur of earlier times with a stunning series of period room settings and Painted Gallery. Changing displays highlight local history and the Costume Gallery features fashions. Broad Street.

ENTERTAINMENT

◆ Casinos - G Casino, Exchanger Row. Rainbow Casino, Summer Street. Soul Casino, Union Street.

◆ Cinemas - 10 Ship Row. 49 Belmont Street. Union Square, Guild Street. Queen's Link Leisure Park (E of Aberdeen).

◆ Concerts - Aberdeen Exhibition and Conference Centre, Bucksburn (NW of Aberdeen). Aberdeen Music Hall, Union Street. Lemon Tree, 5 West North Street.

◆ Theatres - Aberdeen Arts Centre & Theatre: ACT, King Street. His Majesty's Theatre, Rosemount Viaduct. Lemon Tree (as above).

SPORT & LEISURE

◆ Ice Rink - Linx Ice Arena, Beach Promenade (E of Aberdeen).

◆ Parks & Gardens - Union Terrace Gardens, Union Terrace.

◆ Sports Centres - Beach Leisure Centre, Beach Promenade (E of Aberdeen). Chris Anderson Stadium, Linksfield Road. Torry Youth & Leisure Centre, Oscar Road (S of Aberdeen).

◆ Swimming Pools - Beach Leisure Centre (as above).

◆ Tennis Centre - Westburn Tennis Centre, Westburn Park, Westburn Road (W of Aberdeen).

◆ Ten-Pin Bowling - Codonas Amusement Park, Beach Boulevard (E of Aberdeen).

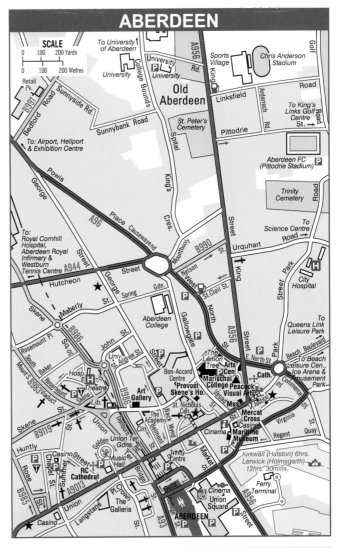

Aberdeen

Marischal College

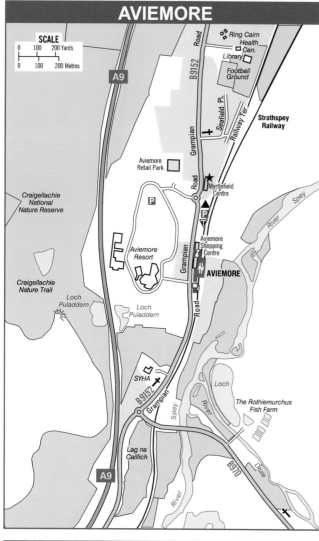

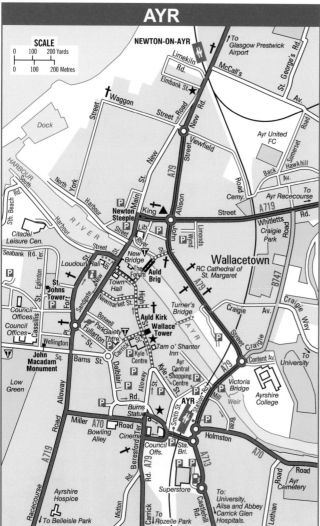

AVIEMORE

32 miles South of Inverness on the A9 lies the Highland resort of Aviemore, a picturesque village renowned for its spectacular mountain scenery. In close proximity to Britain's premier ski area, the Cairngorm Mountains, Aviemore is an ideal base from which to tour the Highlands offering the tourist a diverse range of quality accommodation along with leisure facilities, visitor attractions and an annual programme of events.

PLACES OF INTEREST

Visit Scotland Information Centre (All year) - 12 Grampian Road. PH22 1RH. Tel: (01479) 810930

◆ CRAIGELLACHIE NATIONAL NATURE RESERVE & NATURE TRAIL - (Scottish National Heritage) 260 hectare National Nature Reserve containing a mixture of birchwood and moorland.

◆ STRATHSPEY RAILWAY - 9.5 mile standard gauge railway running between Aviemore, Boat of Garten and Broomhill passing within sight of some of the highest and most spectacular mountains in Scotland. Aviemore Station.

SPORT & LEISURE

◆ Skiing Facilities - The Ski & Snowboard School, Cairngorm Mountain, 9 miles SE of Aviemore.

AYR

Ayr is a busy shopping centre and commercial seaport. With its long stretches of sandy beach, backed by pleasant lawns behind the esplanade, it is also one of Scotland's premier coastal resorts. The town is centred around Alloway Street and High Street. Famous for its associations with Burns (born in Alloway immediately to the south and who described Ayr as the town of 'honest men and bonnie lasses'), the Tam O'Shanter Inn on the High Street & 'Twa Brigs' (Auld Brig, described below, and New Bridge built in 1788, rebuilt in 1877-9) feature in his works. Burns statue is near the railway station in Burns Statue Square. Of architectural interest are the restored 16th century Loudoun Hall on Boat Vennel off New Bridge Street, the oldest building in the town, and the Town Buildings surmounted by a slender spire built in the early 1820s, off the same road. Ayr Racecourse (in the east of the town) is Scotland's top horse racing centre.

PLACES OF INTEREST

Visit Scotland Information Centre (All year) - 22 Sandgate. KA7 1BW. Tel: (01292) 290300

◆ AULD BRIG - Bridge over River Ayr dating from c1470, subject of Burns' 'Twa Brigs'. For 300 years Ayr's only bridge, now pedestrianized. High Street / River Street.

◆ AULD KIRK - Fine church, also known as the New Church of St John, built in 1655 with money given by Cromwell to replace the 'Old Church' (see below) incorporated in his fort. Kirk Port, High Street.

◆ JOHN MCADAM MONUMENT - Monument to John McAdam, the road builder, born in Ayr in 1756, who gave his name to the word 'tarmacadam'. Wellington Square.

◆ NEWTON STEEPLE - Georgian steeple of 1795, the former entrance to parish church. Newton-on-Ayr. King Street.

◆ ST JOHN'S TOWER - Restored tower of Old Church of St John where the Scottish Parliament met after Bannockburn in 1315 to confirm the future of the Scottish Crown. Later absorbed into a large Cromwellian fort built in 1652. Views to island of Arran from top. By appointment. Bruce Crescent.

◆ WALLACE TOWER - Early 19th century neo-gothic tower, with statue of William Wallace in niche, built on site where Wallace, the Scottish patriot, is reputed to have been imprisoned in the early 1300s. High Street.

ENTERTAINMENT

◆ Cinemas - Burns Statue Square.

◆ Concerts - Town Hall, New Bridge Street. Gaiety Theatre, Carrick Street. Citadel Leisure Centre, South Harbour Street.

◆ Theatres - Gaiety Theatre (as above).

SPORT & LEISURE

◆ Parks & Gardens - Belleisle Park, Belleisle (S of Ayr). Craigie Park, Craigie Road. Low Green, Wellington Square. Rozelle Park, Monument Road (S of Ayr).

◆ Sports Centres - Citadel Leisure Centre, South Harbour Street.

◆ Swimming Pools - Citadel Leisure Centre (as above).

◆ Ten-Pin-Bowling - LA Bowl, Miller Road.

DUMFRIES

Dumfries is an attractive border town situated on the picturesque River Nith that divides it from Maxwelltown, with which it was amalgamated in 1929. With many of the houses painted in pastel colours or built of Lochar Briggs red sandstone and a modern shopping centre, it is the main centre for the region being given the status of a royal burgh as early as the 12th century. The town was the scene of the murder of 'the Red' Comyn by Robert Bruce in 1306 (marked by a plaque on a building in Castle Street), an event that started a change in the course of Scottish history that culminated with the defeat of the English at the battle of Bannockburn in 1314. Dumfries has been sacked many times, notably by the retreating Bonnie Prince Charlie in 1745 after his march on England, and consequently there is little from the medieval period to see, however a walk along the High Street and the waterfront at Whitesands is recommended. The Academy on Academy Street educated the playwright and novelist James Matthew Barrie, author of 'Peter Pan' whilst Robert Burns, Scotland's national poet lived here between 1791 and his death in 1796 during which time he wrote many of his poems and songs. The town contains many Burns sites of interest including (in addition to those listed below) a plaque marking his first home in Bank Street (then called Wee Vennel or 'Stinking Vennel' by Burns because of an open sewer which ran down the street to the river), a marble statue in front of Greyfriars church, Castle Street (built in 1867) and his family pew in St Michael's church, St Michael Street. Burns' favourite walk (now called 'Burns' Walk'), is on the east bank of the river off Nunholm Road in the north of the town.

PLACES OF INTEREST
Visit Scotland Information Centre (All year) - 64 Whitesands. DG1 2RS.
Tel: (01387) 253862
◆ BURNS MAUSOLEUM - Built in 1815 in the style of a domed Grecian temple. Burns, his wife & several of his children are buried here. St Michael's Churchyard, St Michael Street.
◆ DEVORGILLA BRIDGE (OLD BRIDGE) - Six arched sandstone bridge of 1431, rebuilt in the 17th century after severe flood damage, now pedestrianized. Last in a succession of bridges here; the first wooden structure was built by Lady Devorgilla Balliol in the 13th century. Mill Road / Whitesands.
◆ DUMFRIES CAMERA OBSCURA - Astronomical instrument (one of only three in Scotland) installed in 1836 on the top floor of the old windmill tower at Dumfries Museum. Moving panoramic images are projected onto a table top screen allowing visitors to enjoy magnificent views of Dumfries & the surrounding countryside in a unique way. Dumfries Museum, The Observatory, Rotchell Road.
◆ DUMFRIES MUSEUM - History of South West Scotland. Exhibitions trace the history of the people of Solway, Dumfries & Galloway, early Christianity, prehistory, natural history & Victorian life. The Observatory, Rotchell Road.
◆ GLOBE INN - 17th century working inn; Burns' favourite tavern. Rooms retain their 1790's look, memorabilia includes the poet's chair. 56 High Street.
◆ GRACEFIELD ARTS CENTRE - Large collection of Scottish paintings. Monthly exhibitions of contemporary art & craft. 28 Edinburgh Road.
◆ MID STEEPLE - Old Town Hall (or tolbooth) built between 1707 & 1708 marking the town centre. A table shows distances to important Scottish towns & to Huntingdon in England. High Street.
◆ OLD BRIDGE HOUSE MUSEUM - Museum of local life in sandstone building built in 1660 (the oldest house in Dumfries) adjoining Devorgilla Bridge. Period rooms include a Victorian nursery, kitchens from the mid 19th century & dentist's surgery. Devorgilla Bridge, Mill Road.
◆ ROBERT BURNS CENTRE - Set in an 18th century watermill, audio-visual presentations, exhibitions, original manuscripts & relics recount Burns' last years in Dumfries. The centre also includes a model of Dumfries in Burns' time, museum trails, activities for children, plus an award-winning café-restaurant. In the evenings the centre is home to the regional film theatre for Dumfries & Galloway. Mill Road.
◆ ROBERT BURNS HOUSE - Refurbished 18th century sandstone house, Burns' second home which he moved to in 1793 & where he died in 1796 at the age of thirty-seven, containing his writing desk & chair, manuscripts & relics connected with the poet. Burns Street.

ENTERTAINMENT
◆ Cinemas - Shakespeare Street. Robert Burns Film Theatre, Robert Burns Centre (as above).
◆ Concerts - Easterbrook Hall, The Crichton Site, Bankend Road (SE of Dumfries).
◆ Theatres - Easterbrook Hall (as above). Theatre Royal, Shakespeare Street.

SPORT & LEISURE
◆ Ice Rinks - Dumfries Ice Bowl, King Street.
◆ Parks & Gardens -Castledykes Park, Glencaple Road (S of Dumfries). Deer Park, Mill Road. Dock Park, St Michael's Bridge Road. Goldie Park, Glasgow Street. Greensands, Park Lane. Hamilton Stark Park, Moat Road (S of Dumfries). King George V Park, Glasgow Street. Mill Green, Mill Road. Noblehill Park, Annan Road (E of Dumfries).
◆ Sports Centres - David Keswick Athletic Centre, Marchmount (NE of Dumfries). DG One Leisure Complex, Hoods Loaning. (closed for renovation). King George V Sports Complex, King George V Park, Glasgow Street.

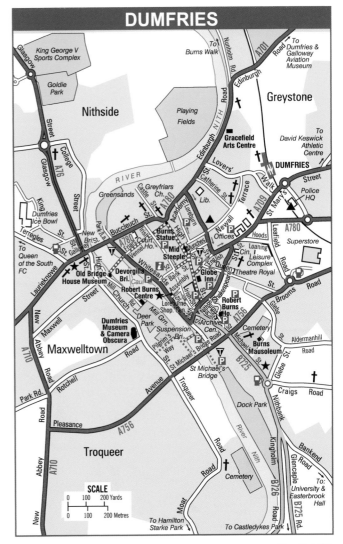

Devorgilla Bridge

Loch Ken

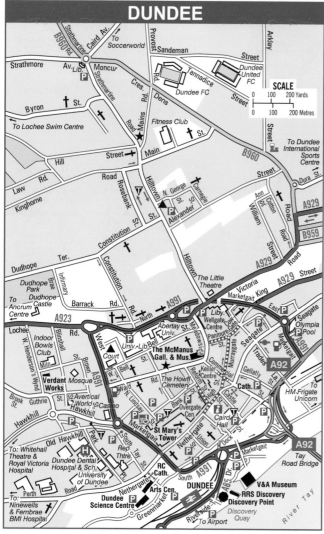

DUNDEE

With its picturesque setting on the River Tay, Dundee is the fourth largest city in Scotland. The history and fortunes of Dundee are inextricably linked to its maritime heritage. Dundee was once the United Kingdom's leading whaling port and maritime trading meant that goods from around the world were available. The emphasis on sea trading meant that ship construction was an important industry and today great vessels such as the RRS Discovery and HM Unicorn a three masted frigate of 1824 survive to reflect a vital part of Dundee's heritage. By the early 19th century the textile industry was thriving and Dundee became renowned as the jute capital of the world. Of historical interest Dundee has much to offer, The Howff, which was for three centuries until 1857 the city's primary burial ground, was given to the town in 1564 by Mary Queen of Scots. However, originally it was an adjoining orchard to a Franciscan monastery founded in 1270 by Devorguilla Balliol and destroyed in 1548.

Wishart Arch located on Cowgate is thought to date from 1548 and is the only surviving city gate. It is named in memory of George Wishart, a reformer who was burnt at St Andrews in 1546. During 1544, when Dundee was stricken by plague, Wishart preached from this gate in two directions; to those affected who were excluded from the town and those within whom remained unaffected. 1878 saw the construction of the Tay Rail Bridge, which at two miles long was the longest bridge in the world. However, it was not to be long before disaster struck and on the evening of December 28th the following year during a severe storm, the centrepiece of the bridge collapsed while a train was crossing it which resulted in the death of the 75 passengers on board. Engineering faults and poor construction were blamed for the disaster but this did not deter from reconstructing it, a project that commenced three years after the tragedy.

Today Dundee is a lively city to explore where industrial heritage has laid the foundations for an exciting range of modern tourist attractions. It is a popular University City, with a large student community it offers a vibrant nightlife. An exciting waterfront regeneration programme is currently under way including housing, hotels, leisure and retail facilities. The skyline will include a new Victoria & Albert Museum, a landmark stone building on the bank of the River Tay.

PLACES OF INTEREST

Visit Scotland Information Centre (All Year) - City Square. DD1 3BG
Tel: (01382) 527527

◆ DISCOVERY POINT & RRS DISCOVERY - Attraction centres around Captain Scott's famous Antarctic exploration ship, which was built in Dundee in 1901. Dramatic visual presentations recreate the events in the Discovery story and other exhibitions reveal what happened to the ship following the exploration. Discovery Quay.

◆ DUDHOPE CASTLE - Dating from the 13th century, the castle was once the hereditary home of the Constables of Dundee. Used as offices by Dundee City Council (Exterior view only) Barrack Road.

◆ DUNDEE CATHEDRAL - Dating from 1853, this Scottish Episcopal Church was designed by Sir George Gilbert Scott. The Cathedral's 64 m (210 ft) high tower and spire is a renowned landmark. High Street.

◆ DUNDEE CONTEMPORARY ARTS - A hub for the contemporary art scene, the DCA houses five floors of galleries, cinemas, artists facilities, education resources and the Café Bar. 152 Nethergate.

◆ DUNDEE ROMAN CATHOLIC CATHEDRAL - This Cathedral church dedicated to St Andrew was designed in the Gothic style and dates from 1836. Nethergate.

◆ DUNDEE ST MARY'S TOWER - The 15th century tower known also as the "Old Steeple" is the only surviving part of the pre-Reformation Church of St Mary. Nethergate.

◆ DUNDEE SCIENCE CENTRE - This innovative science centre offers an insight into the perception of the senses using state of the art displays and interactive exhibits. Gift shop and coffee shop. Greenmarket.

◆ MCMANUS GALLERIES & MUSEUM, THE - Housed in a Victorian Gothic building dating from 1867 is Tayside's main regional museum and art gallery. It houses a fine array of exhibits including collections of silver, glass and furniture. There are displays on local history and a fine art collection which includes the work of Scottish artists from the 19th and 20th centuries. Albert Square.

◆ VERDANT WORKS - This restored 19th century jute mill is one of a few surviving examples of the industry. Exhibitions reveal how Dundee became the jute capital of the world and the effect that the industry had in shaping the town's history. West Henderson's Wynd.

◆ V&A MUSEUM OF DESIGN - Showcasing Scottish design elements from the V&A collections and international touring exhibitions within a stunning waterfront building. (Opening 2018).

ENTERTAINMENT

◆ Casinos - Grosvenor Casino, West Marketgait. ◆ Cinemas - Douglas Road (NE of Dundee). Kingsway West (NW of Dundee). Dundee Contemporary Arts, Nethergate. ◆ Concerts - Caird Hall, City Square.
◆ Theatres - Dundee Repertory Theatre, Gardyne Theatre, Gardyne Road (E of Dundee). Tay Square. The Little Theatre, Victoria Road. Whitehall Theatre, Bellfield Street (W of Dundee).

SPORT & LEISURE

◆ Climbing Walls - Avertical World, Blinshall Street. ◆ Parks & Gardens - Dudhope Park, Dudhope Terrace. ◆ Ski Slope - Ancrum Outdoor Centre, Ancrum Road (NW of Dundee). ◆ Sports Centres -Dundee International Sports Centre, Mains Loan (NE of Dundee). ◆ Swimming Pools - Lochee Swim

Dundee Museum

Arbroath Cliffs

Forth Rail Bridge

Loch Lomond

DUNFERMLINE

Scotland's ancient capital for over 500 years, Dunfermline was one of the early settlements of the Celtic Church and a favoured stronghold of the warrior King Malcolm Canmore. In 1070 King Malcolm married the saintly Saxon princess, Margaret whom while fleeing from the Normans was shipwrecked in the Forth and taken to Dunfermline. Together they founded their palace and later built a priory. In 1270 following her death, Margaret was proclaimed a saint and Dunfermline became one of the great centres of pilgrimage in Europe. The town is associated with the birth of numerous kings and queens and is the final resting place of Robert the Bruce. Aside from royalty, Dunfermline has benefited significantly from the generosity of Andrew Carnegie, the great philanthropist who did much to improve facilities available to the people of his native town. Today Dunfermline is a bustling town with a wealth of history to be discovered and a diverse range of visitor attractions.

PLACES OF INTEREST

Visit Scotland Information Centre (All Year) - 1 High Street. KY12 7DL.
Tel: (01383) 720999

◆ ABBOT HOUSE HERITAGE CENTRE - Located in the historic Maygate, the award-winning Abbot House takes the visitor through 1000 years of history from the Picts to the present day. Café, gift shop and garden. Maygate.

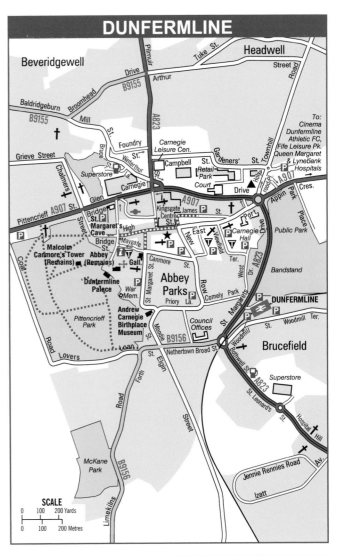

◆ ANDREW CARNEGIE BIRTHPLACE MUSEUM - Located in the house where Carnegie was born in 1835, the museum tells the extraordinary story of his rise from poverty to prominence when he emigrated to the United States and created the country's largest steel works. On the first Friday of every month visitors are able to enjoy demonstrations of a working Jacquard handloom reminiscent of the one used by Carnegie's father. The Memorial Hall, endowed by Mrs Louise Carnegie, adjoins the birthplace cottage and charts her husband's astounding business career from bobbin boy to the world's richest steel magnate. Touch-screen displays. Shop & café. Moodie Street.

◆ DUNFERMLINE ABBEY - (Historic Scotland) Remains of a Benedictine abbey founded by Margaret I in the 11th century. The foundations remain under the present Romanesque style nave built during the 12th century. A brass in the choir marks the grave of King Robert the Bruce. Pittencrieff Park.

◆ DUNFERMLINE CARNEGIE LIBRARY AND GALLERIES - Opened in 2017 this building contains a museum, exhibition areas and library. The museum tells the story of Dunfermline's past through films, computer games and exhibits including home settings from different eras from the 20th century. Café. 1-7 Abbot Street.

◆ DUNFERMLINE PALACE - (Historic Scotland) Royal Palace developed out of the original abbey guest house. The palace was destroyed by fire in 1304 but was rebuilt by James IV in 1500. It was the birthplace of Charles I, the last monarch born in scotland in 1600. Pittencrieff Park.

◆ MALCOLM CANMORE'S TOWER - Ruin of a fortified tower alongside the burn where King Malcolm Canmore held court after the death of Macbeth. Pittencrieff Park.

◆ ST MARGARET'S CAVE - 84 steps below the Glen Bridge Car Park is the cave where Margaret, an 11th century queen and saint sought refuge for prayer and meditation. Glen Bridge Car Park.

ENTERTAINMENT

◆ Cinemas - Fife Leisure Park (NE of Dunfermline).
◆ Concerts - Carnegie Hall, East Port.
◆ Theatres - Carnegie Hall (as above).

SPORT & LEISURE

◆ Parks & Gardens - Dunfermline Public Park, Appin Crescent. McKane Park, Limekilns Road. Pittencrieff Park, Pittencrieff Street.
◆ Sports Centres - Carnegie Leisure Centre, Pilmuir Street.
◆ Swimming Pools - Carnegie Leisure Centre (as above).

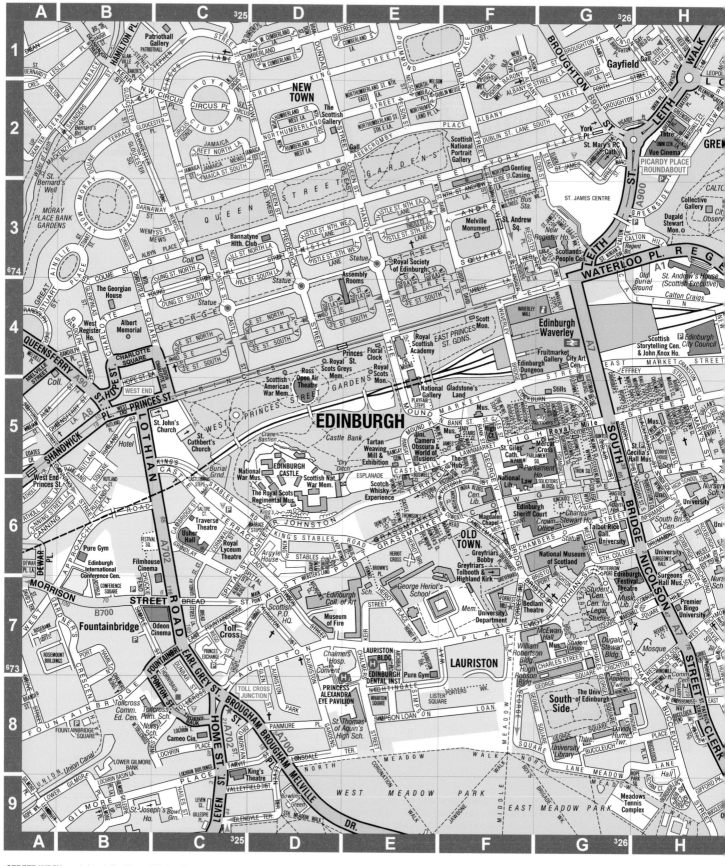

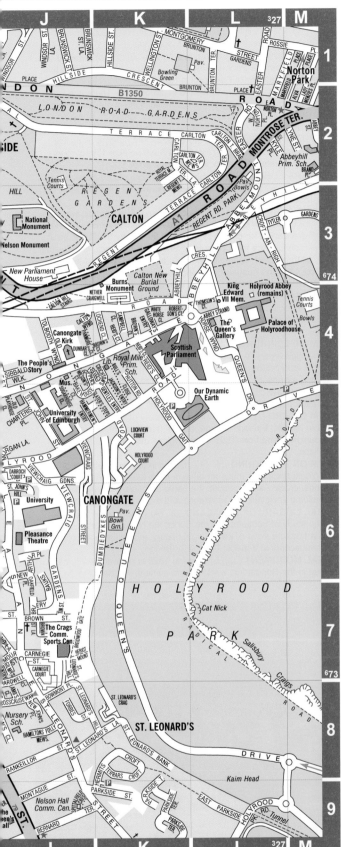

REFERENCE

One-way Street — Traffic flow on A Roads is also indicated by a heavy line on the driver's left.	
Junction Name	WEST END
Restricted Access	
Pedestrianized Road	
Track & Footpath	
Residential Walkway	
Railway	Station ⟷ Tunnel
Edinburgh Trams	Stop
Built-up Area	ALBYN PL.
Car Park (selected)	P
Church or Chapel	†
Fire Station	■
Hospital	H
House Numbers (A & B Roads only)	70 / 65

Visit Scotland Information Centre	i
National Grid Reference	325
Police Station	▲
Post Office	★
Toilet	▽
Educational Establishment	
Hospital or Healthcare Building	
Industrial Building	
Leisure or Recreational Facility	
Place of Interest	
Public Building	
Shopping Centre or Market	
Other Selected Buildings	

SCALE : 1:9504 (6.66 inches to 1 mile)

0 — ¼ — ½ MILE
0 — 250 — 500 — 750 Metres

Index

Hutton Rd. —4K
Hyndford's Cl. —5H

India Bldgs. —6F
India Pl. —2B
India St. —2C
Infirmary St. —6H
Inglis Ct. —6E

Jackson's Cl. —5G
Jackson's Entry —4K
Jamaica M. —2C
Jamaica St. —2C
(not continuous)
Jamaica St. Nth. La.
—2C
Jamaica St. Sth. La.
—2C
James' Ct. —5F
James Craig Wlk. —3G
Jawbone Wlk. —9F
Jeffrey St. —4G
Johnston Ter. —6D

Keir St. —7E
Kerr St. —1B
Kincaid's Ct. —6G
King's Stables La. —6D
King's Stables Rd.
—5C
Kyle Pl. —2L

Lady Lawson St. —6D
Lady Menzies Pl. —2M
Lady Stairs Cl. —5F
Lady Wynd —6D
Lamb's Cl. —8J
Lauriston Gdns. —7D
Lauriston Pk. —7D
Lauriston Pl. —7D
Lauriston St. —7D
Lauriston Ter. —7E
Lawnmarket —5F
Leamington Rd. —9A
Leith St. —3G
Leith Wlk. —2H
Leopold Pl. —1H
Leslie Pl. —1A
Leven Cl. —9C
Leven St. —9C
Leven Ter. —8D
Lister Sq. —8E
Lit. King St. —3H
Lochend Cl. —4K
Lochrin Basin La. —9B
Lochrin Bldgs. —8C
Lochrin Pl. —8C
Lochrin Ter. —8C
Lochview Ct. —5K
London Rd. —1H
Lonsdale Ter. —8D
Lothian Rd. —5B
Lothian St. —7G
Lwr. Gilmore Bank
—8B
Lwr. Gilmore Pl. —9A
Lyne St. —2M
Lyon's Cl. —5G

Mackenzie Pl. —2A
Main Point —7D
Market St. —5F
Marshall's Ct. —3J
Marshall St. —7G
Maryfield —2L
Maryfield Pl. —2L

Meadow La. —8G
Melville Dr. —9D
Melville Pl. —4A
Melville St. —5A
Merchant St. —6F
Meuse La. —4F
Middle Mdw. Wlk. —9F
Milne's Ct. —5E
Montague St. —9J
Montgomery St. —1L
Montgomery St. La.
—1H
Montrose Ter. —2L
Moray Pl. —3B
Morrison's Cl. —5H
Morrison St. —7A
Mound, The —4E
Mound Pl. —5E
Multrees Wlk. —3F

Nelson Pl. —2E
Nelson St. —2E
Nether Craigwell —4K
New Arthur Pl. —6J
New Broughton —1F
New John's Pl. —8J
New Skinner's Cl. —5H
New St. —4H
Nicolson Sq. —7H
Nicolson St. —6H
Niddry St. —5G
Niddry St. Sth. —6H
Nightingale Way —8E
Nth. Bank St. —5F
North Bri. —4G
Nth. Bri. Arc. —5G
Nth. Castle St. —3C
Nth. Charlotte St. —4B
Nth. Clyde St. La. —2F
North E. Circus Pl.
—2C
Nth. Gray's Cl. —5H
North Mdw. Wlk. —8D
Nth. Richmond St.
—6H
Nth. St Andrew La.
—3F
Nth. St Andrew St.
—2F
Nth. St David St. —3E
Northumberland Pl.
—2E
Northumberland Pl. La.
—2E
Northumberland St.
—2D
Northumberland St.
Nth. East La. —2E
Northumberland St.
Nth. West La. —2D
Northumberland St.
Sth. East La. —2E
Northumberland St.
Sth. West La. —2D
North West Circus Pl.
—2B
North West
Cumberland St. La.
—1D

Old Infirmary La. —6H
Old Playhouse Cl. —5J
Old Tolbooth Wynd
—4J
Omni Cen. —2H

Paisley Cl. —5H
Panmure Cl. —4J
Panmure Pl. —8D
Parkside St. —9K
Parkside Ter. —9K
Parliament Sq. —5F
Patriothall —1B
Picardy Pl. —2G
Playfair Steps —5E
Pleasance —6J
Ponton St. —8C
Porters Wlk. —8F
Port Hamilton —7B
Portsburgh Sq. —6D
Potterrow —7G
Potterrow Port —6G
Princes Exchange —7C
Princes Mall —4F
Princes St. —5B

Quarry Cl. —8H
Queen's Dr. —4L
Queensferry St. —4A
Queensferry St. La.
—5A
Queen St. —3C
Queen St. Gdns. East
—2E
Queen St. Gdns. West
—3D

Radical Rd. —6L
Ramsay Gdn. —5E
Ramsay La. —5E
Randolph Cres. —4A
Randolph La. —4B
Randolph Pl. —4B
Rankeillor St. —8J
Reekie's Ct. —7H
Regent Rd. —3H
Regent Ter. —3K
Regent Ter. M. —3K
Register Pl. —3F
Reid's Cl. —4K
Reid's St. —4K
Richmond La. —7H
Richmond Pl. —6H
Riddle's Ct. —5F
Riego St. —7C
Robertson's Cl. —6H
Robertson's Ct. —4K
Rope Wlk. —9A
Rosebank Cotts. —7A
Rosemount Bldgs.
—7A
Rose St. —4C
Rose St. Nth. La. —4C
(not continuous)
Rose St. Sth. La. —4C
(not continuous)
Rossie Pl. —1L
Roxburgh Pl. —6H
Roxburgh's Cl. —5F
Roxburgh St. —6H
Royal Cir. —2C
Royal Ter. —2H
Royal Ter. M. —2K
Rutland Ct. La. —6B
Rutland Pl. —5B

Rutland Sq. —5B
Rutland St. —5B

St Andrew Sq. —3F
St Bernard's Cres.
—1A
St Colme St. —4B
St David's Ter. —7A
St Giles St. —5F
St James Cen. —3G
St James Pl. —2G
St James Sq. —3G
St John's Hill —6J
St John St. —5J
St Leonard's Bank
—8K
St Leonard's Crag
—8K
St Leonard's Hill —7J
St Leonard's La. —8J
St Leonard's St. —8J
St Mary's St. —5H
St Ninian's Row —4J
St Patrick Sq. —8H
St Patrick St. —8H
St Stephen Pl. —1B
St Stephen St. —1B
St Vincent Pl. —1C
St Vincent St. —1C
Saltire Ct. —6C
Saunders St. —2B
Scotsman Bldgs. —5G
Semple St. —7B
Shandwick Pl. —5A
Simon Sq. —7H
Simpson Loan —8E
Slater's Steps —5K
Solicitors Bldgs. —6G
South Bri. —5G
Sth. Charlotte St. —4C
Sth. College St. —6G
South East Circus Pl.
—2C
South East Cumberland
St. La. —1D
Sth. Gayfield La. —1H
Sth. Gray's Cl. —5H
South Mdw. Wlk. —9D
South St Andrew St.
—3F
South St David St.
—3F
South West
Cumberland St. La.
—1D
Spittalfield Cres. —9J
Spittal St. —7C
Spittal St. La. —6D
Stafford St. —5A
Stevenlaw's Ct. —5H
Sugarhouse Cl. —5J
Surgeon's Hall —6H

Tarvit St. —8C
Terrars Cft. —8K
Teviot Pl. —7F
Thistle Ct. —3E
Thistle St. —3D
Thistle St. Nth.
East La. —3E
Thistle St. Nth.
West La. —3D
Thistle St. Sth.
East La. —3E
Thistle St. Sth.
West La. —3D

Thomson's Ct. EH1
—6E
Thomson's Ct. EH8
—4L
Thorny Bauk —7C
(not continuous)
Tron Sq. —5G
Trunk's Cl. —5H
Tweeddale Ct. —5H
Tytler Gdns. —3L

Union Path —9A
Union Pl. —2H
Union St. —1G
Upper Bow —5F
Up. Dean Ter. —2A
Up. Gilmore Pl. —9B
Up. Greenside La. —2H

Valleyfield St. —9C
Vennel —6E
Victoria St. —6F
Victoria Ter. —6F
Viewcraig Gdns. —5J
Viewcraig St. —5J

Warden's Cl. —6F
Wardrop's Ct. —5F
Warriston's Cl. —5F
Waterloo Pl. —3G
Waverley Bri. —4F
Waverley Steps —4G
Webster's Land —6D
Wellington St. —1K
Wemyss Pl. —3C
Wemyss Pl. M. —3B
W. Adam St. —6H
West App. Rd. —7A
West Bow —6F
West College St. —6G
West Crosscauseway
—8H
West End —5B
W. Nicolson St. —7H
W. Norton Pl. —2L
W. Parliament Sq. —5F
West Port —7D
W. Register St. —3F
W. Register St. La.
—3F
W. Richmond St. —7H
West Tollcross —8C
White Horse Cl. —4K
William St. —5A
Wilson's Ct. —4J
Windmill Cl. —8H
Windmill La. —8H
Windmill Pl. —7H
Windmill St. —8G
Windsor St. —1J
Windsor St. La. —1J
World's End Cl. —5H

York La. —2G
York Pl. —2F
Young St. —4C
Young St. Nth. La.
—4C
Young St. Sth. La.
—4C

Fountainbridge Sq.
—8B
Fountain Cl. —5H
Frederick St. —3D

Gabriel's Rd. —3G
Galloway's Entry —4K
Gardner's Cres. —7B
Gayfield Cl. —1H
Gayfield Sq. —1H
Geddes Entry —5G
Gentle's Entry —5K
George IV Bri. —5F
George Sq. —8G
George Sq. La. —8F
George St. —4C
Gibbs Entry —7H
Gifford Pk. —9H
Gillespie Pl. —9C
Gillespie St. —9B

Gilmore Pk. —9A
Gilmore Pl. —9B
Gilmore Pl. La. —9B
Gilmour's Cl. —6E
Gilmour's Entry —7J
Gilmour St. —7J
Glanville Pl. —1B
Glenfinlas St. —4B
Glengyle Ter. —9C
Glen St. —8D
Gloucester La. —2B
Gloucester Pl. —2B
Gloucester Sq. —2B
Gloucester St. —2B
Grassmarket —6E
Gray's Ct. —7H
Gt. King St. —2D
Gt. Stuart St. —4A

Greenside End —2H
Greenside La. —2H
Greenside Pl. —2H
Greenside Row —3H
Greyfriars —6F
Greyfriars Pl. —6F
Grindlay St. —6C
Grindlay St. Ct. —7C
Grove St. —8A
Gullan's Cl. —5H
(not continuous)
Guthrie St. —6G

Haddon's Ct. —7H
Hailes St. —9C
Hamilton Folly M.
—8J
Hamilton Pl. —1B
Hammermen's Entry
—5J

Hanover St. —3E
Hardwell Cl. —7J
Hart St. —1G
Hart St. La. —1G
Hastie's Cl. —6G
Haugh St. —1B
Heriot Bri. —6E
Heriot Cross —6E
Heriot Mt. —7J
Heriot Pl. —7E
Heriot Pl. —7H
Heriot Row —3C
Hermits Cft. —8K
High Riggs —7C
High School Wynd
—6H
High School Yards
—6H
High St. —5F
Hill Pl. —7H
Hill St. —3D
Hillside Cres. —1J

Hillside St. —1K
Hill Sq. —6H
Hill St. —3C
Hill St. North La. —3C
Hill St. South La.
—4C
Holyrood Cl. —5K
Holyrood Gait —5K
Holyrood Pk. Rd.
—9L
Holyrood Rd. —5J
Home St. —8C
Hope Pk. Sq. —8H
Hope St. —5B
Hope St. La. —5B
Horse Wynd —4L
Howden St. —7H
Howe St. —2D
Hunter's Cl. —6E
Hunter Sq. —5G

EDINBURGH

Referred to as the 'Athens of the North', Edinburgh is a flourishing city renowned for its history, style, diversity and prestigious annual festival, which is considered to be the most important and successful event of its kind in Britain. During the month of August, the city becomes a magnet for thousands of people from around the world intent on participating in the festival scene.

Edinburgh divides itself between the Old and New Town areas. The Old Town includes the ancient city centre, where the famous Royal Mile links the Castle and Holyrood, and the historical districts of Grassmarket and Greyfriars. The New Town, dating mainly from the 18th century extends north from Princes Street, Edinburgh's main shopping street, and comprises a continuous development of grand streets, squares, circuses and green spaces regarded as a masterpiece of urban architecture.

PLACES OF INTEREST

Visit Scotland Information Centre (All year), (4G 74) - 3 Princes Street. EH2 2QP. Tel: 0131 473 3868. www.edinburgh.org

◆ **CAMERA OBSCURA & WORLD OF ILLUSIONS** (5E 74) - This Victorian 'Eye in the Sky' has fascinated visitors for 150 years with its live moving panorama of the city. Enjoy access to free telescopes showing a spectacular 360° rooftop panorama and listen to your guide recount tales of Edinburgh's exciting past. In World of illusions you can immerse yourself in five floors of mind-boggling hands-on exhibits from shadow walls to bendy mirrors, seeing in 3D to shaking hands with your ghost. Gift shop. Castlehill.

◆ **CITY ART CENTRE** (4G 74) - A rich collection of fine art, almost entirely by Scottish artists, is housed within the six floors of the City Art Centre. The galleries display a wide range of media, including painting, drawing, print, sculpture, photography and installation art. Café and shop. 2 Market Street.

◆ **EDINBURGH CASTLE** (5D 74) - (Historic Scotland). The imposing fortress of Edinburgh Castle has dominated the cityscape since the Middle Ages, defiantly rooted to the ancient volcanic outcrop upon which it stands. Its strategic positioning and defensive structures have withstood countless sieges and provided successive Kings and Queens with refuge. The castle is home to the Scottish Crown Jewels, the Stone of Destiny and the famous 15th century siege gun Mons Meg. Of particular note is the remarkable St Margaret's Chapel, which has remained perfectly intact for 900 years, making it Edinburgh's oldest surviving building. Castlehill.

◆ **EDINBURGH DUNGEON, THE** (4F 74) - Experience 500 years of the capital's most blood-curdling history. Live actors, two hair-raising rides, shows and special effects transport visitors back to life in barbaric times. Market Street.

◆ **FLORAL CLOCK** (4E 74) - In 1903, John McHattie, the city's Park Superintendent, conceived the idea of the Floral Clock. The face and hands of the working clock are carpeted with thousands of small plants, all of which are replanted in Spring & Autumn. Princes Street.

◆ **FRUITMARKET GALLERY** (4G 74) - Exhibiting contemporary art of the highest quality, the gallery is committed to bringing the work of artists with both established and emerging international reputation to Scotland and presenting the work of Scottish artists. 45 Market Street.

◆ **GEORGIAN HOUSE** (4B 74) - (National Trust for Scotland) Situated on the north side of Charlotte Square, designed by Robert Adam in 1791, this house exemplifies the style of Edinburgh's New Town architecture. The rooms of No.7 (built in 1796) are furnished in period style. There is a video presentation "Living in a Grand Design" that reflects life in the New Town. The "Below Stairs" life of servants is also illustrated. Charlotte Square.

◆ **GLADSTONE'S LAND** (5F 74) - (National Trust for Scotland) Once the home of a wealthy merchant, this six-storey tenement building along the Royal Mile has been authentically restored to illustrate how 17th century people lived and worked. Gift shop. 477B Lawnmarket.

◆ **GREYFRIARS BOBBY** (6F 74) - Statue in memory of Greyfriars Bobby, the skye terrier who watched over his master's grave for 14 years after his death from 1858-1872. Candlemaker Row.

◆ **HOLYROOD ABBEY** (4L 75) - (Historic Scotland) The ruined nave is all that remains of this Abbey church founded for Augustinian canons during the late 12th and early 13th centuries. Beneath the Abbey the Royal Vault was the final resting place for a number of Scottish Kings, including David II (son of Robert the Bruce), James II, James V and Lord Darnley, Mary Queen of Scot's second husband. Canongate.

◆ **MUSEUM OF CHILDHOOD** (5H 74) - This museum houses an extensive collection of childhood memorabilia including toys, games, books and dolls. For the adult visitor there are exhibitions relating to the history of child welfare including health, education and upbringing. Gift shop. 42 High Street.

◆ **MUSEUM OF EDINBURGH** (4J 75) - A series of 16th to 18th Century buildings arranged around a close, provide the setting for exhibitions devoted to the local history of Edinburgh. The diverse range of artefacts include pottery, silverware, street signs and treasures of national importance. Watch the city evolve at your feet in Foundation Edinburgh, the museum's latest blacked-out theatre attraction. Gift shop. 142 Canongate.

◆ **MUSEUM OF FIRE** (7D 74) - Relating the history of the oldest municipal fire brigade in the UK. Exhibits include manual horse drawn, steam & motorised pumps dating from 1806 & fire engines dating from 1910. Lauriston Place.

◆ **MUSEUM ON THE MOUND** (5F 74) - Based in the headquarters of Scotland's oldest bank, this museum takes a fresh look at money; see a million pounds, crack a safe, or build the bank! Displays illustrate the story of banks, building societies, life assurance and more. North Bank Street.

◆ **NATIONAL LIBRARY OF SCOTLAND** (6F 74) - The world's foremost centre for the study of Scotland and the Scots, the National Library of Scotland is a treasure trove of knowledge, history and culture with millions of books, manuscripts and maps. George IV Bridge.

◆ **NATIONAL MONUMENT** (3J 75) - Built in 1826 to honour the Scottish who perished in the Napoleonic wars, this monument was designed to

View from Edinburgh Castle

emulate the Parthenon, (temple dedicated to Athena, the Greek goddess of war). Unfortunately, it was never completed due to a collapse in funding and remains today unfinished. Calton Hill.

◆ **NATIONAL MUSEUM OF SCOTLAND** (6G 74) - Extensively re-developed in 2011, to include 16 galleries with displays exploring Scottish history, the natural world, world cultures, science and technology and art and design. With a wealth of interesting objects from fossils to future technology, meteorites to deep sea creatures, canoes to musical instruments and bicycles to space age rockets. Chambers Street.

◆ **NATIONAL WAR MUSEUM OF SCOTLAND** (5D 74) - This absorbing museum detailing 400 years of Scottish military history, reflects the experience of war, sourced from personal diaries, photographs and official documents. Other exhibits include uniforms, insignia and equipment, medals, decorations, weapons, paintings, ceramics and silverware. Edinburgh Castle.

◆ **NELSON MONUMENT** (3J 75) - Built between 1807 and 1815, this was one of the first monuments to Admiral Nelson. The climb to the top is rewarded with splendid panoramic views across the city. Exhibition, telling the story of the monument's history & the Battle of Trafalgar. 32 Calton Hill.

◆ **OUR DYNAMIC EARTH** (5K 75) - Through technology including a 3D and 4D experience, discover our planet's past, present and future. Be shaken by volcanoes, fly over glaciers, feel the chill of polar ice, get caught in a tropical rainstorm and debate the planet's future. A new gallery is planned, in which an interactive exhibition commemorates the life of James Hutton known as "The father of geology". 107 Holyrood Road.

◆ **PALACE OF HOLYROODHOUSE & HOLYROOD PARK** (4L 75) - At the eastern end of Edinburgh's historic Royal Mile stands the Palace of Holyroodhouse, the Queen's official Scottish residence. Today, tourists can visit the Royal apartments, the Throne room, the Royal Dining Room and the Great Gallery to experience the grandeur of this Royal residence. Changing exhibitions throughout the year. Canongate, Royal Mile.

◆ **PEOPLE'S STORY, THE** (4J 75) - Housed in the 16th century Tolbooth, this museum reflects working class life in Edinburgh since the 18th century. Sounds, sights, smells and reconstructed rooms combine to evoke an atmosphere of a bygone era. Canongate Tolbooth.

◆ **REID CONCERT HALL MUSEUM OF INSTRUMENTS** (7G 74) - An outstanding and diverse collection of over 1000 musical instruments from around the world chronicling the art of instrument making over the past 400 years. Changing exhibitions throughout the year. Bristo Square.

◆ **ROYAL SCOTS REGIMENTAL MUSEUM, THE** (6D 74) - The visitor is taken back to the raising of the regiment in 1663 and with displays of maps, tableaux and dioramas the story of the regiment is told, right up to the present day. Castlehill.

◆ **ROYAL SCOTTISH ACADEMY** (4E 74) - Presenting the cream of Scottish contemporary art through an on-going programme of exciting exhibitions including painting, sculpture, printmaking, installation, photography, architecture, new media, film and performance art. The Mound.

◆ **ST. CECILIA'S HALL MUSEUM OF INSTRUMENTS** (5H 74) - St. Cecilia's Hall was built in 1763 and is the oldest concert hall in Scotland. On display are 50 highly important and well-preserved early keyboard instruments. There is also a display of harps, lutes, citterns and guitars. Cowgate.

◆ **ST. GILES' CATHEDRAL** (5F 74) - Founded in 1120, the mother church of Presbyterianism, most of the remaining architecture dates from the 14th and 15th centuries including the famous crown spire that dominates the city skyline. Royal Mile.

◆ **ST. MARY'S RC CATHEDRAL** (2G 74) - This Cathedral church of St. Mary was designed by James Gillespie Graham and dates from 1814 and 1890. The St. Andrews Altar contains the National Shrine to Scotland's patron saint. Broughton Street.

◆ **SCOTCH WHISKY EXPERIENCE, THE** (6E 74) - Enjoy a ride through history in a whisky barrel to discover the traditions and origins of whisky production. Hear stories recounting the magical craft and let the experts advise you on the perfect dram for your palate. 345 Castlehill.

◆ **SCOTTISH NATIONAL GALLERY** (5E 74) - Located in the heart of the city, the gallery has been open to the public since 1859. The collection comprises a comprehensive catalogue of work from the Renaissance era to the Post Impressionist period. The Mound.

◆ **SCOTTISH NATIONAL PORTRAIT GALLERY** (2F 74) - Visual history of Scotland from the 16th century to the present day depicted through portraits of figures who shaped it: royalty, philosophers, poets and rebels are included. The gallery also houses the National Collection of Photography. 1 Queen Street.

◆ **SCOTTISH PARLIAMENT** (4K 75) - Standing boldly at the eastern end of the historic Royal Mile, the new building is open to visitors Monday to Saturday. Take a free guided tour and learn about the work, history and procedures of the Scottish Parliament, as well as the design and architecture of this striking building. Canongate.

◆ **SCOTTISH STORYTELLING CENTRE** (5H 74) - Programme of live performances, visual arts & workshops celebrating Scotland's storytelling heritage. Also included in this attraction is John Knox House, associated with dramatic events in Scotland's turbulent history. James Mosman, goldsmith to Mary Queen of Scots, once lived here. 43-45 High Street.

◆ **SCOTT MONUMENT** (4F 74) - One of Edinburgh's most famous

Edinburgh Tattoo

landmarks, this monument to Sir Walter Scott is 200 ft high and dates from 1840. The 287 steps lead to stunning panoramic views over the city centre. East Princes Street Gardens.

◆ **STILLS GALLERY** (5G 74) - Scotland's premier photographic gallery exhibits a comprehensive collection of contemporary photography. 23 Cockburn Street.

◆ **SURGEONS' HALL MUSEUMS** (6H 74) - Originally developed as a teaching museum for students of medicine and first opened to the public in 1832, the building houses one of the largest and most historic collections of surgical pathology material in the United Kingdom. It can also lay claim to being Scotland's oldest museum. Permanent displays include the Pathology Museum, the History of Surgery and the Dental Museum. Nicolson Street.

◆ **TALBOT RICE GALLERY** (6G 74) - Based at the University of Edinburgh, the Talbot Rice Gallery is one of Scotland's leading public galleries of contemporary visual art. South Bridge.

◆ **TARTAN WEAVING MILL AND EXHIBITION** (5E 74) - Housed in the former Castlehill Reservoir Cistern, this working mill allows visitors to view the entire production process of tartan from sheep to kilt. 555 Castlehill.

◆ **WRITERS' MUSEUM** (5F 74) - Located in the historic Lady Stair's House dating from 1622, the museum houses an exhibition that revolves around Scotland's three great writers; Robert Burns, Sir Walter Scott and Robert Louis Stevenson. Lady Stair's Close.

The following attractions are located outside the city centre map
◆ Arthur's Seat (Holyrood Park) 1 ½ miles South East of city centre.
◆ Royal Botanic Garden (Inverleith Row) 1 mile North of city centre.
◆ Royal Yacht Britannia (Leith Docks) 2 ½ miles North of city centre.
◆ Scottish National Gallery of Modern Art (Belford Road) 2 miles West of city centre.

ENTERTAINMENT
◆ Cinemas - Greenside Place. Home Street. 2 Lothian Road.
◆ Concerts - Assembly Rooms, George Street. Edinburgh Festival Theatre, Nicholson Street. Edinburgh Playhouse, Greenside Place. Queens Hall, Clerk Street. Ross Open Air Theatre, Princes Street Gardens. Usher Hall, Lothian Road.
◆ Theatres - Edinburgh Festival Theatre (as above). Edinburgh Playhouse (as above). King's Theatre, Leven Street. Royal Lyceum Theatre, Grindlay Street. Traverse Theatre, Cambridge Street.
LEISURE
◆ Parks & Gardens - Calton Hill, Regent Road. East Meadow Park, Meadow Lane. East and West Princes Street Gardens, Princes Street. Holyrood Park, Queen's Drive. London Road Gardens, London Road. Moray Place Bank Gardens, Moray Place. Queen Street Gardens, Queen Street. Regent Gardens, Regent Terrace. Regent Road Park, Abbeymount. West Meadow Park, Melville Drive.

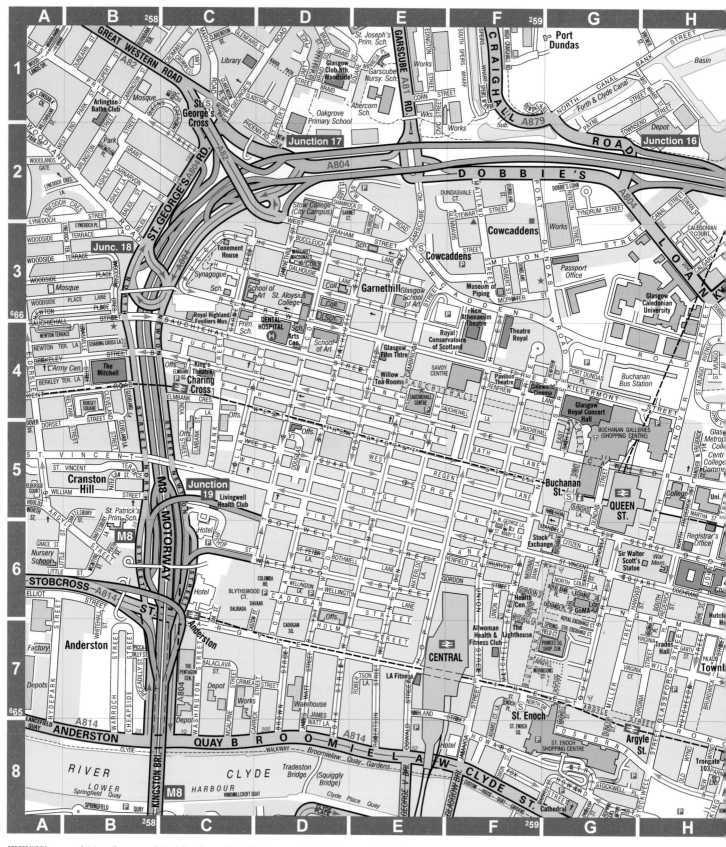

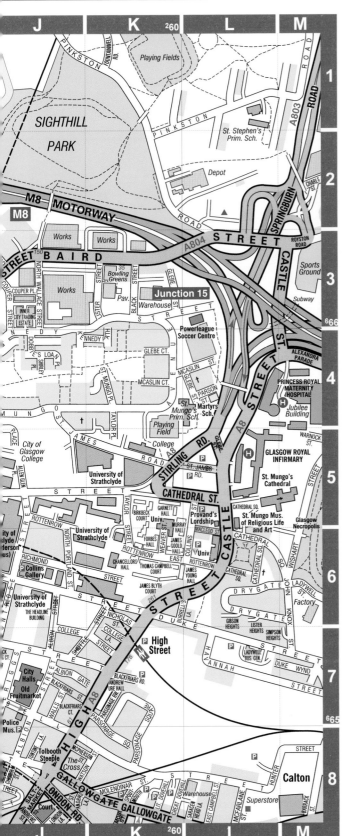

REFERENCE

One-way Street Traffic flow on A Roads is also indicated by a heavy line on the driver's left.	
Junction Name	DOBBIE'S LOAN INTERCHANGE
Restricted Access	
Pedestrianized Road	
Track & Footpath	
Residential Walkway	
Railway	Station / Tunnel
Subway Station	Ⓢ
Built-up Area	CLYDE PL
Car Park (selected)	P
Church or Chapel	†
Fire Station	■
Hospital	Ⓗ
House Numbers (A & B Roads only)	70 / 65

Visit Scotland Information Centre	i
National Grid Reference	³25
Police Station	▲
Post Office	★
Safety Camera with Speed Limit Fixed cameras and long term road works cameras Symbols do not indicate camera direction	⑳
Toilet	▽
Educational Establishment	
Hospital or Healthcare Building	
Industrial Building	
Leisure or Recreational Facility	
Place of Interest	
Public Building	
Shopping Centre or Market	
Other Selected Buildings	

SCALE : 1:9504 (6.66 inches to 1 mile)

0 ¼ ½ MILE

0 250 500 750 Metres

George Square

GLASGOW

The history of Glasgow can be dated from the 6th century when a settlement developed around the church built by St Mungo on the banks of the Molendinar burn. His popularity earned him the name 'dear one' and to this day is the patron saint of the city. These first inhabitants named their settlement 'Glas Ghu' (dear green place) and with the city and its environs boasting no less than 70 parks and green spaces it certainly lives up to its name. In the period between the death of St Mungo and the granting of a charter in 1175 by William the Lion, little is known of the city's history, but from this date the city became a prosperous centre. In 1451 the university was founded making it Scotland's second oldest after St. Andrew's and the 4th oldest in the UK and in 1611 Glasgow became a Royal Burgh. The city prospered through its ability to trade in tabacco, sugar and cotton with the American colonies but when the American Revolution affected this in 1775 the city turned to industry. With the advent of Industrialisation in the 19th century, Glasgow concentrated upon ship building and soon established a reputation for quality throughout the world that earned the city its reputation as 'Second City of the British Empire.' However, the onset of economic depression in post war England would contribute to the decline of industrial prestige. Depression of the industry was slowed down by the need for naval re-armament in the 1930s but by the 1950s demand was dwindling and combined with cheap foreign competition, Glasgow could no longer compete in the industrial arena.

With a rich heritage of cultural splendour, Glasgow realised that this was the key to renewed prosperity. Splendid Victorian architecture lay beneath the grime of an industrial age and once restored would revive the city as a cultural centre. Many of the city's buildings reflect the style of the talented Glasgow born architect, Charles Rennie Mackintosh (1868-1928) whose influential style contributed significantly to shaping the distinctive forms of Art Nouveau throughout Europe. Architecture became a focus for his artistic expression and in the city there is an abundance of public buildings, private buildings and tea rooms that display the familiar Mackintosh style. The Willow Tea Rooms on Sauchiehall Street, designed for Kate Cranston in 1903 have been restored to reflect Mackintosh's original design and the School of Art on Renfrew Street, architecturally one of Mackintosh's greatest achievements is still in use as an art school. In 1990 Glasgow was awarded the prestigious title of Cultural Capital of Europe and in 1999 was designated UK City of Architecture and design. Today, Glasgow is one of the UK's most visited cities offering visitors a wealth of cultural heritage and visitor attractions.

PLACES OF INTEREST

Visit Scotland Information Centre (All Year), (6G 78) - Gallery of Modern Art, Royal Exchange Square. G1 3AH Tel: 0845 859 1006

◆ **CENTRE FOR CONTEMPORARY ARTS** (4D 78) - Inspiring and cutting edge centre for visual and performance art, film, music, and the spoken word. Housing six major Scottish and international exhibitions over a year. 350 Sauchiehall Street. ◆ **COLLINS GALLERY** (6J 79) - Affiliated to the University, the gallery mounts various exhibitions including contemporary, fine and applied art and photography. 22 Richmond Street. ◆ **GALLERY OF MODERN ART** (6G 78) - Elegant, neo-classical building situated in the heart of the city, the gallery offers a range of contemporary exhibitions and activities, displaying work by Scottish and International artists as well as addressing contemporary social issues. Café. Royal Exchange Square.
◆ **GLASGOW CITY CHAMBERS** (6H 78) - Built in 1883-88 by William Young, the imposing City Chambers is a magnificent example of 19th century architecture that occupies the east side of George Square. Today, they are occupied by Glasgow City Council. George Square. ◆ **GLASGOW NECROPOLIS** (5M 79) - Adjacent to the Cathedral, this cemetery dating from 1883 is modelled on the famous Pere la Chaise in Paris and is renowned for its elaborate tombs. (Pre-booked tours - visit www.glasgownecropolis.org). Castle Street. ◆ **GLASGOW POLICE MUSEUM, THE** (7J 79) - Through the use of text boards and artefacts, the founding and history of the Glasgow Police is presented, along with a section on Police forces from around the world which includes insignia, headgear and uniforms. Bell Street. ◆ **GLASGOW ST ANDREW'S RC CATHEDRAL** (8G 78) - Built 1814-1817 to meet the needs of the growing Catholic population in Glasgow, the Cathedral was later considered "one of the finest ecclesiastical edifices in the city" and is one of the earliest examples of Gothic Revival architecture in the city. It is home to the Archbishop of Glasgow, the most important Roman Catholic figure in Scotland. Dunlop Street. ◆ **GLASGOW ST MUNGOS CATHEDRAL** (5L 79) - (Historic Scotland) Dating predominantly from the 15th century, the cathedral is regarded as one of Glasgow's most important buildings both architecturally and historically. (Guided tours). Castle Street.
◆ **LIGHTHOUSE, THE - SCOTLAND'S CENTRE FOR ARCHITECTURE, DESIGN & THE CITY** (7F 78) - Seeking to promote the disciplines of architecture and design throughout Scotland and abroad, the centre has attracted national and international recognition for its exhibition programmes. Also within the complex is the Mackintosh Interpretation Centre, which provides an insight into the work of the great Scottish artist. Café. 11 Mitchell Lane. ◆ **MITCHELL LIBRARY, THE** (4B 78) - Founded in 1874, this is one of the largest public reference libraries in Europe. Contained within its volumes can be found a wide range of literature relating to the culture and history of Glasgow and Scotland. North Street.

Glasgow University

◆ **MUSEUM AT THE NATIONAL PIPING CENTRE** (3F 78) - Museum houses an outstanding collection of bagpipes and exhibitions that trace the origins and history of piping through innovative displays. (Pre-booked tours - Tel: 0141 353 0220 or visit www.thebagpipeshop.co.uk). 30-34 McPhater Street. ◆ **PROVAND'S LORDSHIP** (5L 79) - Dating from 1471, this is the oldest house in Glasgow which was originally built as a manse to the adjacent St Nicholas Hospital. 3 Castle Street. ◆ **ROYAL HIGHLAND FUSILIERS REGIMENTAL MUSEUM** (3C 78) - Extensively refurbished in 2013 there are displays of medals, uniforms and records relating to the history of The Royal Scots Fusiliers, The Highland Light Infantry and the Royal Highland Fusiliers. 518 Sauchiehall Street. ◆ **ST MUNGO MUSEUM OF RELIGIOUS LIFE & ART** (5L 79) - Innovative museum offering an insight into religious faiths throughout the world through various art forms which aspire to promote understanding and respect between people of different faiths and of none. After exploring the world's major religions visitors can relax in contemplation in the peaceful Zen garden, the first of its kind in Britain. Changing exhibitions. Café. 2 Castle Street. ◆ **SCOTT'S STATUE** (6H 78) - The first monument erected to the great writer Sir Walter Scott (1771-1832). The stone carving dates from 1837. George Square.
◆ **TENEMENT HOUSE** (3C 78) - (National Trust for Scotland) Dating from the late 19th century, this is a typical example of a Victorian tenement flat. Many of the original furnishings remain to create a fascinating insight of life in the early part of the 20th century. 145 Buccleuch Street. ◆ **TOLBOOTH STEEPLE** (8J 79) - Dating from 1626, this seven storey tower with its distinctive crown at the summit of the 34 m (113 ft) high steeple marked the centre of Glasgow until Victorian times. Glasgow Cross. ◆ **TRADES HALL** (7H 78) - One of the most historic buildings in the city. Explore the Grand Hall and discover how the trade houses shaped the Glasgow of today. (Guided tours on Tuesdays). 85 Glassford Street. ◆ **TRONGATE 103** (8H 78) - A resource for the city, housed in an Edwardian warehouse. The centre spans six floors with a print studio, photoworks and two floors of galleries. Café Trongate.

The following attractions are located outside the city centre map
◆ Burrell Collection (Pollok Country Park) 3 miles SW of city centre.
◆ Glasgow Science Centre (Pacific Quay) 2 miles SW of city centre.
◆ Hunterian Museum (University of Glasgow) 2 miles NW of city centre.
◆ Kelvingrove Art Gallery & Museum (Argyle St.) 2 miles W of city centre.
◆ People's Palace (Glasgow Green) 1 mile SE of city centre.
◆ Riverside Museum (Pointhouse Place) 2 1/2 miles W of city centre.
◆ Scottish Exhibition & Conference Centre (SECC) (Exhibition Way) 1 1/2 miles W of city centre.
◆ The Tall Ship at Riverside (River Clyde) 2 1/2 miles W of city centre.

ENTERTAINMENT
◆ Cinemas - Glasgow Film Theatre, Rose Street. Renfrew Street.
◆ Concerts - Glasgow Royal Concert Hall, Sauchiehall Street. City Halls & Old Fruitmarket, Candleriggs. ◆ Theatres - King's Theatre, Bath Street. New Athenaeum Theatre (within Royal Conservatoire), Renfrew Street. Pavilion Theatre, Renfield Street. Theatre Royal, Hope Street. Tron Theatre, Trongate.

SPORT & LEISURE
◆ Parks & Gardens - Sighthill Park, Pinkston Road. ◆ Swimming Pools - North Woodside Leisure Centre, Braid Square.

FALKIRK

The history of Falkirk begins with the arrival of the Romans in the first century AD. The area was once of strategic importance and this is illustrated by the construction of the Antonine Wall, the route of which (now largely obliterated) ran through the centre of Falkirk. Built in 140AD and named after the Roman Emperor of the time, Antonius Pius, who ordered its construction as a defence against the Northern tribes, the Antonine Wall (announced a UNESCO World Heritage Site in 2008) stretched for 36 miles from Old Kirkpartrick on the Clyde to Carriden on the Firth with forts interposed every 2 miles. The wall itself was a turf rampart on a stone base with a ditch to the north and a military road running parallel along the south side. The most significant remains around Falkirk can be viewed in Callendar Park (see below) and to the west of the town on Anson Avenue a short section of embankment can be viewed. Falkirks newest addition is the Falkirk Wheel. The Wheel is a boat lift which links the Forth and Clyde Canal at the point of which it lies 35 m (115 ft) below the level of the Union Canal.

PLACES OF INTEREST

Visit Scotland Information Centre (All year) - The Falkirk Wheel, Lime Road. FK1 4RS. Tel: (01324) 620244

◆ ANTONINE WALL - A section of ditch 40 ft wide, 10 ft deep and half a mile in length runs through Callendar Park and is easily visible. Callendar Road. ◆ CALLENDAR HOUSE & PARK - The 170 acres park has a beautiful bloom of spring daffodils and has the Park Gallery in the grounds. Callendar House displays 600 years of Scottish history through interactive displays and an authentic georgian working kitchen which is the centre of the experience. Callendar Road.◆ FALKIRK STEEPLE - The third incarnation of this Falkirk landmark was built in 1814. A part of the 140 ft high structure used to be the town's lockup. High Street.

ENTERTAINMENT

◆ Cinemas - Central Retail Park, Grahams Road. ◆ Concerts - Town Hall, West Bridge Street. ◆ Theatres - Town Hall (as above).

SPORT & LEISURE

◆ Parks & Gardens - Bellsmeadow Park, Bellsmeadow Road. Blinkbonny Park, Gartcows Road. Callendar Park, Callendar Road. Dollar Park, Camelon Road. Victoria Park, Thornhill Road. ◆ Sports Centres - Mariner Leisure Centre, Glasgow Road (W of Falkirk). Woodlands Games Hall, Cochrane Av. ◆ Swimming Pools - Mariner Leisure Centre (as above).

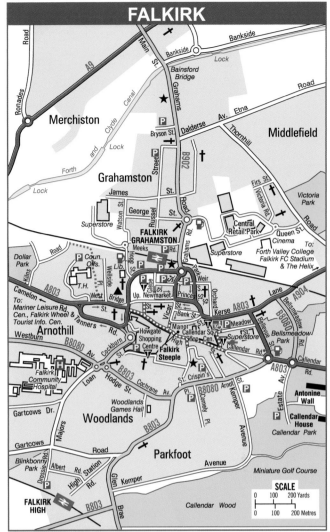

FORT WILLIAM

The history of Fort William can be dated from 1655 when General Monck built an earthwork fort here, the purpose of which to quote Johnson was to keep "savage clans and roving barbarians" at bay. This was later rebuilt under William III and, for a short time the town was renamed Maryburgh in honour of his queen. In both 1715 and 1745, the Jacobites failed to capture the fort and it was eventually pulled down during the late 19th century. For today's visitor, Fort William is synonymous with Ben Nevis and the town has become a popular holiday resort and base for the many people who wish to climb Britain's highest mountain.

PLACES OF INTEREST

Visit Scotland Information Centre (All Year) - 15 High Street. PH33 6DH Tel: (01397) 701801.

◆ JACOBITE, THE (FORT WILLIAM TO MALLAIG STEAM SERVICE) - Considered to be one of the 'greatest railway journeys of the world' the train travels the 84 miles round trip from Fort William to the West Coast fishing port of Mallaig and back. Steeped in history, the route encompasses breathtaking scenery with views of Ben Nevis, Britain's most westerly mainland railway station Ari Saig, Neptune's Staircase and the magnificent 21 arch Glenfinnan Viaduct. Fort William Station.

◆ LIME TREE GALLERY - A privately funded gallery showing both national touring exhibitions and local contemporary artists. Achintore Road.

◆ WEST HIGHLAND MUSEUM - Founded in 1922, exhibitions illustrate the history of traditional Highland life. The museum also houses a world famous Jacobite collection. Cameron Square.

◆ WEST HIGHLAND WAY - Long distance footpath covering 95 miles between Glasgow and Fort William.

ENTERTAINMENT

◆ Concerts - The Nevis Centre, An Aird.
◆ Theatres - The Nevis Centre (as above).

SPORT & LEISURE

◆ Sports Centres - Lochaber Leisure Centre, Belford Road. The Nevis Centre, An Aird.
◆ Swimming Pools - Lochaber Leisure Centre (as above).
◆ Ten Pin Bowling - The Nevis Centre (as above).

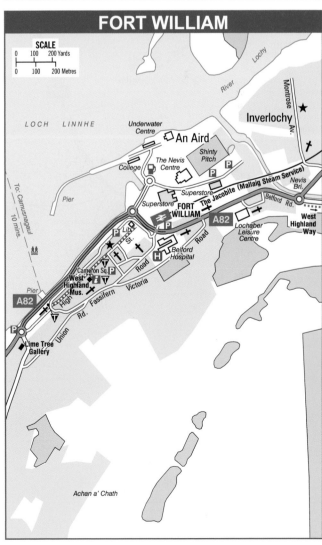

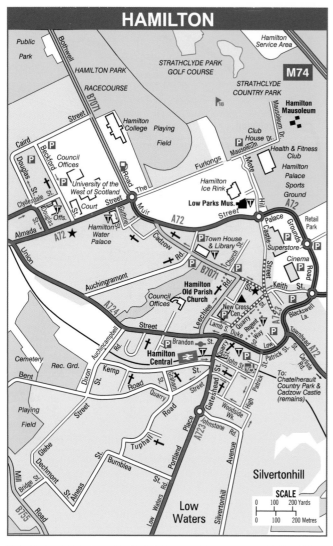

HAMILTON

There has been a settlement at Hamilton since prehistoric times, which was known as Cadzow, a name derived from the Celtic "Cadihou" meaning "beautiful castle." It was in 1445, that a charter granted by James II to the first Lord Hamilton gave permission for the official name of the town to be changed to that of his family. The town was once one of the main stopping places for the stagecoach that ran between England and Scotland and the town's museum (see below) is housed in a former coaching inn. With the rise of industrialisation, the town became the centre of a mining district, but closure of the pits forced diversification and today Hamilton is a thriving town that offers a number of visitor attractions and leisure facilities.

PLACES OF INTEREST

◆ HAMILTON MAUSOLEUM - Built in 1850 for the 10th Duke of Hamilton as a family chapel and crypt at an estimated cost of £150,000 the mausoleum is a spectacular structure designed by David Bryce. Tours booked with Low Parks Museum (see below). Strathclyde Country Park.
◆ HAMILTON OLD PARISH CHURCH - Dating from 1732-34, this church was designed by William Adam. Strathmore Road.
◆ HAMILTON PARK RACECOURSE - Considered to be one of the most picturesque racecourses in Britain, it once formed part of the Royal forest of Cadzow. The inaugural race meeting at Hamilton was held in August 1782 and today the racecourse offers a varied fixture list throughout the season that includes some evening meetings during the summer months. Bothwell Road.
◆ LOW PARKS MUSEUM - Museum was created through the amalgamation of the former District Museum with the Cameronians Regimental Museum and is housed in one of the town's oldest buildings, once a coaching inn which dates from 1696. Exhibitions include displays on the Clyde Valley and Hamilton Estate. 129 Muir Street.

ENTERTAINMENT
◆ Cinemas - Palace Grounds Road.
◆ Concerts - Town House, Cadzow Street.
◆ Theatres - Town House (as above).

SPORT & LEISURE
◆ Ice Rink - Hamilton Ice Rink, Muir Street.
◆ Parks & Gardens - Chatelherault Country Park (SE of Hamilton). Public Park, Bothwell Road. Strathclyde Country Park, The Furlongs.
◆ Sports Centres - Hamilton Palace Sports Ground, Mote Hill.
Hamilton Water Palace, Almada Street.
◆ Swimming Pools - Hamilton Water Palace (as above).
◆ Ten-Pin Bowling - Cosmic Bowl, M & D's Theme Park (NE of Hamilton).

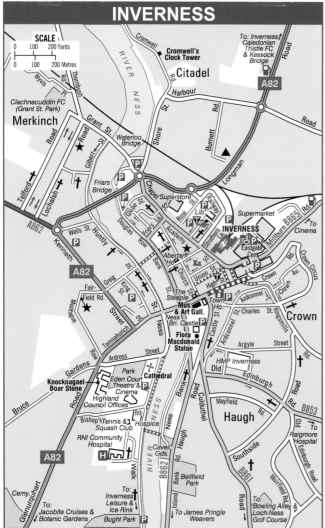

INVERNESS

For many years referred to as the 'Capital of the Highlands', Inverness became a city at the start of the new millennium and has therefore attained the status befitting its title. It is a bustling centre with a rich heritage and though the emphasis today lies with administration, commerce and industry, Inverness is still a worthy tourist destination. Lying on the shores of the Moray Firth and divided by the River Ness, the main part of the town occupies the right bank. Notable buildings include the magnificent castle, built in the 1830s which houses the Sheriff's Court, the Town House, a Victorian Gothic building dating from 1880, Abertarff House, built in 1592 which was restored by the National Trust for Scotland in 1963 and was until recently their highland office and Dunbar's Hospital, built in 1688 as an almshouse. Acting as a green oasis, the Ness Islands, linked by bridges, are a public park which also provide an alternative method of crossing the river where lies the Caledonian Canal, which runs from Fort William to Inverness and dates from 1822.

PLACES OF INTEREST

Visit Scotland Information Centre (All Year) - 36, High Street IV1 1JQ.
Tel: (01463) 252401
◆ CROMWELL'S CLOCK TOWER - Site of Cromwell's Fort which was destroyed during the Restoration, the clock tower is all that remains. Cromwell Road.
◆ FLORA MACDONALD STATUE - This statue dedicated to the Jacobite heroine dominates the grounds of Inverness Castle. Inverness Castle. ◆ INVERNESS CASTLE - The current castle was built of red sandstone in 1836 by William Burn to replace the original which was destroyed by a fire in 1746. Overlooking the River Ness it is now the Sheriff's Court. Only the grounds are open to the public. Castle Street. ◆ INVERNESS CATHEDRAL - Built from red sandstone between 1866 & 1869, this gothic style cathedral was the first to be completed in Britain after the reformation. Lack of funding meant they were unable to add the planned 30 m spire. Ardross Street. ◆ INVERNESS MUSEUM & ART GALLERY - Displays of human and natural history are combined to reflect the history of Inverness and the Highlands. The collection also includes silver, weapons and period costume. Café. Castle Wynd. ◆ KNOCKNAGAEL BOAR STONE - Preserved within the Council Offices, the stone is inscribed with Pictish symbols which depict a mirror case and wild boar. Glenurquhart Road.

ENTERTAINMENT
◆ Cinemas - Eastfield Way (E of Inverness). Eden Court Theatre, Bishops Road.
◆ Concerts - Eden Court Theatre (as above). ◆ Theatres - Eden Court Theatre (as above).

SPORT & LEISURE
◆ Ice Rink - Inverness Ice Centre, Bught Park. ◆ Parks & Gardens - Bellfield Park, Island Bank Road. Bught Park (S of Inverness). Northern Meeting Park, Ardross St. Whin Park (S of Inverness). ◆ Sports Centres - Inverness Leisure, Bught Park. ◆ Swimming Pools - Inverness Leisure (as above). ◆ Ten-Pin Bowling - Rollerbowl, Culduthel Road (S of Inverness).

KILMARNOCK

Kilmarnock, a commercial town noted for its pedestrian friendly town centre, is reputed to have derived its name from the early Christian missionary St Marnock but the town only started to grow after receiving a Royal Charter in 1592. It was here that John Wilson (buried in Old High Kirk churchyard) published the first edition of Burns' poems in 1786, the site of his printing shop being marked by a plaque in Burns Precinct off The Cross. Other Burns associations include Laigh Kirk, the former tower remaining with the rebuilt nave of 1802, situated off Bank Street in the oldest surviving part of the town.

PLACES OF INTEREST

◆ BURNS MONUMENT - Monument to the poet with statue erected in 1879. Having been damaged by a fire in recent years, the monument has been redeveloped as the focal point of a new genealogy centre, the Burns Monument Centre. Kay Park, Strawberry Bank Road.
◆ DEAN CASTLE COUNTRY PARK - 200 acre park with visitor centre, walks, rivers, adventure playground and pets corner. Contains Dean Castle, built around a 14th century tower house, containing armour, tapestries, musical instruments and Burns manuscripts. Café. Dean Road.
◆ DICK INSTITUTE - Contains two art galleries and three museum galleries housing both temporary and permanent displays of natural sciences, industrial & local history and fine & contemporary art. Elmbank Avenue.
◆ NISBET STONE - Stone recalling the hanging here of John Nisbet in 1683 for supporting the Covenanters at the battle of Bothwell Bridge. The Cross.
◆ REFORMERS MONUMENT - Corinthian column erected in 1885 to commemorate Scottish pioneers of Parliamentary Reform. Kay Park, Strawberrybank Road.

ENTERTAINMENT

◆ Cinemas - Queen's Drive.
◆ Concerts - Palace Theatre, Green Street.
◆ Theatres - Palace Theatre (as above).

SPORT & LEISURE

◆ Ice Rink - Galleon Leisure Centre, Titchfield Street.
◆ Parks & Gardens - Dean Park, Dean Road. Dean Castle Country Park, Dean Road. Howard Park, Dundonald Road. Kay Park, Strawberrybank Road. Strawberry Gardens, Strawberrybank Road.
◆ Sports Centres - Galleon Leisure Centre (as above). Hunter Fitness Suite, Western Road.
◆ Swimming Pools - Galleon Leisure Centre (as above).
◆ Ten-Pin Bowling - The Garage, Grange Street.

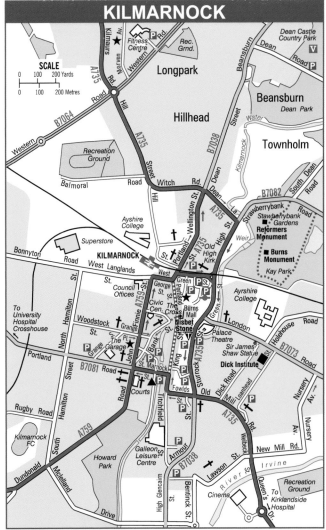

KIRKCALDY

With a historical past dating back to the 11th century, Kirkcaldy has an important industrial heritage. During the 19th century, Kirkcaldy was the first town to use the power loom which would revolutionise the textile industry and it was world renowned for its manufacture of linoleum. Though little remains of this era there is still much to discover around the town. The main street that extends along the waterfront for over 4 miles gave rise to Kirkcaldy becoming known as the 'Lang toun of Fife' and even today it is still referred to as this. In the town centre the Town House dating from 1939-56 is topped by Kirkcaldy's patron, St Bryce. Near the harbour is Sailor's Walk, a row of 17th century houses restored by the National Trust for Scotland. The town has numerous famous associations; it was the birth place of the architect, Robert Adam in 1728 and Adam Smith was born here in 1723, returning later to write his influential work, 'Wealth of Nations'. Thomas Carlyle is also associated with the town for the period he spent teaching at the burgh school. In April Kirkcaldy hosts the famous Links Market along the Esplanade. Incorporating over a mile of fairground attractions and rides, the market dates from 1304 and is considered to be the longest street fair in Britain.

PLACES OF INTEREST

◆ KIRKCALDY GALLERIES - Exhibits a fine collection of 19th & 20th century Scottish paintings, including works by William McTaggart and the Scottish Colourist S J Peploe. The Glasgow Boys are also well represented. There are also fascinating displays of local and natural history, a changing programme of exhibitions, café and shop. War Memorial Gardens. Abbotshall Road.

ENTERTAINMENT

◆ Cinemas - Adam Smith Theatre, Bennochy Road.
◆ Concerts - Adam Smith Theatre (as above).
◆ Theatres - Adam Smith Theatre (as above).

SPORT & LEISURE

◆ Ice Rink - Fife Ice Arena, Rosslyn Street (NE of Kirkcaldy).
◆ Parks & Gardens - Beveridge Park, Abbotshall Road. Ravenscraig Park (NE of Kirkcaldy). War Memorial Gardens, Kirkcaldy Station.
◆ Sports Centres - Kirkcaldy Leisure Centre, Esplanade.
◆ Swimming Pools - Kirkcaldy Leisure Centre (as above).

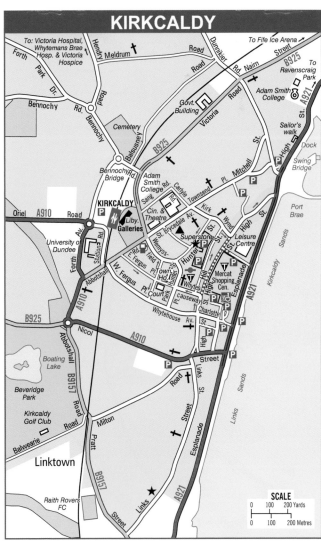

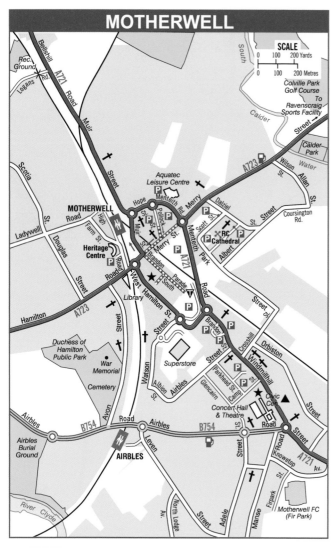

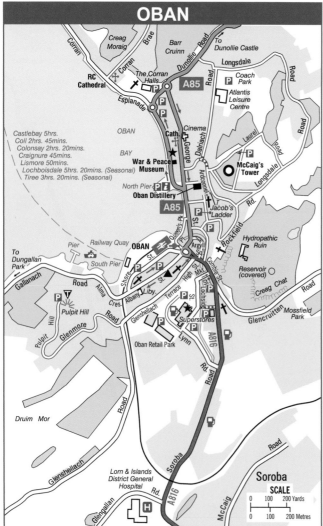

MOTHERWELL

Located at the head of the Clyde Valley, Motherwell is well situated to discover the Upper Clyde Valley, New Lanark World Heritage Site and the beautiful Scottish Borders. The town was once famous for its iron, steel and engineering works and was home to the great Dalzell works, founded in 1871 by David Colville.

PLACES OF INTEREST

◆ MOTHERWELL HERITAGE CENTRE - Multi-media exhibition illustrates the history of Motherwell and the effects of industry on the area from the 19th century to the present day. There is also a fifth floor viewing tower with spectacular views up and down the Clyde Valley and on a clear day Ben Lomond can be seen. High Road.
◆ MOTHERWELL RC CATHEDRAL - Dates from the 1900's and became a cathedral in 1947. Coursington Road.

ENTERTAINMENT

◆ Concerts - Motherwell Concert Hall & Theatre, Windmillhill Street.
◆ Theatres - Motherwell Concert Hall & Theatre (as above).

SPORT & LEISURE

◆ Parks & Gardens - Calder Park, Merry Street. Duchess of Hamilton Public Park, Avon Road. ◆ Sports Centres - Aquatec Leisure Centre, Menteith Road. Ravenscraig Sports Complex (NE of Motherwell). ◆ Swimming Pools - Aquatec Leisure Centre (as above).

Oban Bay

OBAN

Well situated on the shore, flanked by the island of Kerrera which provides protection against Atlantic storms, Oban is regarded as the 'unofficial capital of the West Highlands' and 'The Gateway to the Isles'. The town revolves around its busy port with fishing craft and leisure boats filling the harbour with colour and activity. Since 2010 a bi-annual "Festival of the Sea" has been held in late May to celebrate the importance of the sea to the towns economy. Cruises are an important part of Oban's tourist industry and it is the main port for ferries bound for the Inner Hebrides with numerous other trips available to the islands of Coll, Tiree, Barra, South Uist, Colonsay and Islay. Obscured from view from the bay, the remains of Dunollie Castle to the north of Oban affords stunning views to the harbour by way of a short, but steep walk along a partially hidden path.

PLACES OF INTEREST

Visit Scotland Information Centre (All Year) - North Pier. PA34 5QD.
Tel: (01631) 563122
◆ MCCAIG'S TOWER - This folly dating from 1897 was commissioned by a local banker who aspired to alleviate unemployment whilst simultaneously perpetuating his own name. Though never completed, the tower stands as a monument to the McCaig family and the short walk up Jacobs Ladder to the viewing platform offers an excellent vantage point with outstanding views across the Bay to the Isle of Kerrera. Laurel Road. ◆ OBAN DISTILLERY - Built in 1793, the distillery combines guided tours which reveal the ancient craft of distilling with exhibitions and an audio-visual presentation reflecting the history of Oban. Stafford Street. ◆ OBAN EPISCOPAL CATHEDRAL - Consisting of the original church of 1864 with its partially-built 1910 replacement, the Cathedral has suffered from a lack of funds throughout its existence, yet retains a dignified presence. George St. ◆ OBAN ROMAN CATHOLIC CATHEDRAL - Modern granite building dating from 1932, built by Sir Giles Gilbert Scott. Corran Esplanade. ◆ WAR & PEACE MUSEUM - Collection of artefacts and memorabilia dating predominantly from the Second World War. Learn about the fishing and maritime industries, the railways and local sports such as Shinty. Old Oban Times Building. Corran Esplanade.

ENTERTAINMENT

◆ Cinemas - Phoenix Cinema, George Street. ◆ Concerts - The Corran Halls, Corran Esplanade. ◆ Theatres - The Corran Halls (as above).

SPORT & LEISURE

◆ Parks & Gardens - Dungallan Park, Gallanach Road. Mossfield Park, Glencruitten Road. ◆ Sports Centres - Atlantis Leisure, Dalriach Road.
◆ Swimming Pools - Atlantis Leisure (as above).

PAISLEY

With the White Cart Water flowing through the town centre, Paisley is a constantly developing town that is far more than a satellite of nearby Glasgow. Like so many other towns, Paisley flourished during the 19th century with the Industrial Revolution acting as a catalyst to providing prosperity for the town. British and French soldiers returning from India at the end of the 18th century brought with them fine Kashmir shawls which provided the inspiration for the development of a flourishing industry. The Kashmir designs were copied and Paisley soon became world renowned for its distinctively woven shawls.

PLACES OF INTEREST

◆ COATS OBSERVATORY - Dating from 1883 the displays in the centre offer an insight into the history of astronomy, astronautics and meteorology. 49 Oakshaw Street West.

◆ PAISLEY ABBEY - A Cluniac Abbey Church originally founded in 1163, though destroyed by fire in 1307. The remaining structure dates mainly from the 15th century and within the church is displayed the Barochan Cross, a 10th century Celtic cross which is under the care of Historic Scotland. Abbey Close.

◆ PAISLEY MUSEUM & ART GALLERIES - The museum is home to the world's largest paisley shawl collection. Other exhibitions include displays on local industry and natural history. The Pillar Gallery re-opened in November 2012 following a complete refurbishment. Along with displays of work from Scottish artists and writers there are innovative computer displays and an interactive experience. High Street.

◆ PAISLEY RC CATHEDRAL - Built in 1932 in the neo-romanesque style and replacing the church of 1809, this cathedral church is dedicated to St Mirin, a 17th century Irish abbot who worked, died and was laid to rest here. Incle Street.

◆ PAISLEY THREAD MILL MUSEUM - Housed in part of the Mile End Mill, the collection includes artefacts and photographs of the mills from the 19th and 20th centuries. Seedhill Road.

◆ SMA' SHOT COTTAGES - Experience life in the 18th century in three weaver's cottages furnished in period style and containing the original looms. 2 Sma' Shot Lane.

ENTERTAINMENT

◆ Cinemas - Phoenix Business Park (W of Paisley).
◆ Concerts - Town Hall, Abbey Close.
◆ Theatres - Paisley Arts Centre, New Street. Town Hall (as above).

SPORT & LEISURE

◆ Parks & Gardens - Barshaw Park, Glasgow Road (E of Paisley). Brodie Park, Braids Road (S of Paisley). East End Park, Seedhill Road. Fountain Gardens, Love Street. Saucelhill Park, Hunterhill Road.
◆ Sports Centres - Ferguslie Sports Centre, Blackstoun Road. (W of Paisley). Lagoon Leisure Centre, Christie Street.
◆ Swimming Pools - Lagoon Leisure Centre (as above).

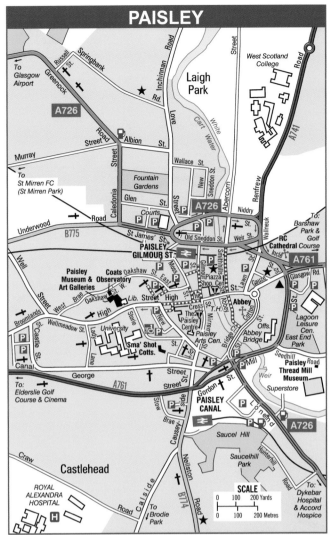

PERTH

Lying on the west bank of the River Tay, the Royal burgh of Perth is thought to have originated from a Roman camp and though there is dispute as to the validity of this, the rectangular street patterns seem to suggest that it may have been. Once the capital of Scotland, Perth was an important centre and coupled with its favourable location on the navigable River Tay, has maintained its pre-eminence as both a favourable tourist destination and busy harbour. There is a rich heritage to be discovered around the town with a diverse range of visitor and recreational attractions. The riverside North Inch Park is the notorious location of the 1396 'Battle of the Clans' when the Chattan and Kay clans fought each other to the death as a result of King Robert III unsuccessful attempt to curtail feuding between Highlanders. It was this battle that inspired Sir Walter Scott's novel, 'The Fair Maid of Perth.'
The annual Perth Festival of the Arts held at the end of May encompasses the whole spectrum of performing arts and is considered to be one of the finest festivals of its kind in Scotland.

PLACES OF INTEREST

Visit Scotland Information Centre (All Year) - 45 High Street. PH1 5TJ
Tel: (01738) 450600

◆ BLACK WATCH REGIMENTAL MUSEUM - Housed in Balhousie Castle, dating from 1860's as it stands, exhibitions illustrate the history of the 42nd / 73rd Highland regiment from 1740 to the present day. Displays include silver, colours, uniforms and medals. Hay Street.

◆ FERGUSSON GALLERY - Former waterworks converted into gallery, devoted to exhibiting the work of Scottish colourist painter, John Fergusson (1874-1961) who was an influential figure in the development of 20th century art in Scotland. Three galleries exhibit changing thematic displays of his work. Marshall Place.

◆ PERTH CATHEDRAL - Episcopal Cathedral founded in 1850 to serve the diocese of St Andrews, Dunkeld and Dunblane. North Methven Street.

◆ PERTH MUSEUM & ART GALLERY - Diverse range of displays covering fine and applied art, local and social history, natural history and archaeology. A changing programme of temporary exhibitions runs throughout the year. 78 George Street.

◆ ST JOHN'S KIRK - Founded in 1126 by David I and with much of the existing building dating from the 15th century, the kirk is the oldest standing building in Perth. John Knox preached here during the Reformation and in later years the kirk was divided into three separate churches, the reunification only occurring in 1923 in memory of the men of Perth who died in WW1. St. John Street.

ENTERTAINMENT

◆ Cinemas - Murray Street. ◆ Concerts - Perth Concert Hall, Mill Street.
◆ Theatres - Perth Theatre, High Street.

SPORT & LEISURE

◆ Ice Rink - Dewars Centre, Glover Street. ◆ Parks & Gardens - Bellwood Park, Dundee Road. North Inch Park, Hay Street. South Inch Park, King's Place.
◆ Sports Centres - Bells Sports Centre, Hay Street. ◆ Swimming Pools - Perth Leisure Pool, Glasgow Road.

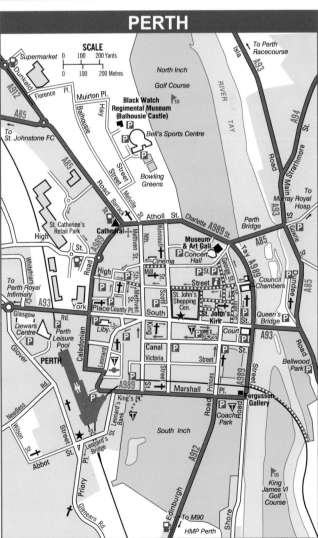

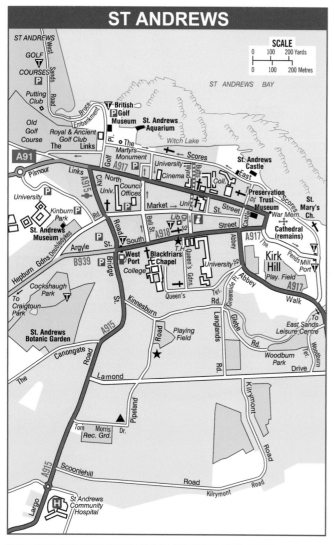

ST ANDREWS

ST ANDREWS

According to legend, the town of St Andrews derives its name from the namesake saint whose remains were brought to this place by St Rule, a Greek monk. It was from here that a settlement developed with Celtic monks building St Mary's Church. The town became an important pilgrimage site with many people making the journey to visit the shrine of St Andrew, who became the patron saint of Scotland.

It is not only as a religious centre that St Andrews is worldly famous; it is heralded as the golfing capital of the world with numerous premier courses interspersed around the area. The game prospered in St Andrews and the Society of St Andrews Golfers was founded in 1754 to organise an annual competition, this later became known as the Royal and Ancient Golf club and today it is recognised as the governing body for the games rules in most countries. Professional and amateur championships also team matches attract golfers from around the world.

Originally a market town, St Andrews was appointed a Royal Burgh in 1620 and is home to the oldest University in Scotland, founded in 1412 by Bishop Henry Wardlaw. St Salvator's on North Street was founded in 1450 and St Leonards dates from 1512 with the two being merged in 1747. St Mary's College founded in 1537 is home to the theology faculty. West Sands, one of Scotland's best beaches and location for some of the scenes in the film Chariots of Fire is also popular with visitors.

PLACES OF INTEREST

Visit Scotland Information Centre (All Year) - 70 Market Street. KY16 9NU. Tel: (01334) 472021

◆ BLACKFRIARS CHAPEL - A vaulted side apse is all that remains of this 1525 chapel that was formerly part of a Dominican friary founded in 1274. South Street.

◆ BRITISH GOLF MUSEUM - The museum presents a chronological exploration of the development of golf spanning the last 500 years. An extensive collection of golfing memorabilia is combined with explanatory displays and innovative exhibitions covering all golfing aspects including tournaments, players and the evolution of golfing equipment. Bruce Embankment.

◆ ST ANDREWS AQUARIUM - The aquatic habitats of the world are explored here, from the crabs, starfish, sharks and octopus of our own seas, to the angelfish, clownfish and poisonous wolf fish from the tropics. Amazonian piranhas, poison dart frogs and hairy spiders are also present. Humbolt Penguins from the warm seas off South America. Seal enclosure pool and observation platform with seal feeding sessions twice a day. Land animals are also represented with a growing family of Meerkats. Gift shop and café. The Scores.

◆ ST ANDREWS BOTANIC GARDEN - Discover a hidden treasure of almost 8000 species of ferns, herbaceous plants, shrubs and trees laid out in different areas including the Water Garden, Rock Garden and Heath Garden. The Canongate.

◆ ST ANDREWS CASTLE - (Historic Scotland) Overlooking the sea are ruins of the 13th century stronghold, once belonging to the Archbishops of St Andrews. Today, notable features that remain include a 24 ft deep bottle dungeon hollowed out of solid rock from which death was allegedly the only escape and a mine and counter mine remaining from a siege in 1546. The visitor centre incorporates a fascinating multi-media exhibition that illustrates the history of the castle. The Scores.

◆ ST ANDREWS CATHEDRAL and ST RULE'S TOWER - (Historic Scotland) Founded in 1160 by Bishop Arnold, this was once the largest cathedral in Scotland and the centre of the medieval Scottish church. The Cathedral museum houses an important collection of Early Christian and medieval artefacts found on the site. The Pends.

◆ ST ANDREWS MUSEUM - Housed in Kinburn House, a Victorian mansion, the museum traces the history of the St Andrews area from the Bronze Age to the present. Doubledykes Road.

◆ ST ANDREWS PRESERVATION TRUST MUSEUM - Collection reflects the social history of the burgh and includes a 1950's reconstruction of a grocery shop with period furniture, photographs and paintings. 12 North Street.

◆ ST ANDREWS WEST PORT - Dating from 1589, with renovations in 1843, this is one of the few remaining city gates in Scotland. Exterior view only. South Street.

◆ ST MARY'S CHURCH - Perched on the cliff edge behind the cathedral, little remains of this cruciform church which was the earliest collegiate church in Scotland. East Scores.

ENTERTAINMENT

◆ Cinemas - New Picture House, North Street.
◆ Concerts - Town Hall, South Street. Younger Hall, Music Centre, University of St Andrews, North Street.

SPORT & LEISURE

◆ Parks & Gardens - Cockshaugh Park, Hepburn Gardens. Craigtoun Park (SW of St Andrews). Kinburn Park, Doubledykes Road. Woodburn Park, Glebe Road.
◆ Sports Centres - East Sands Leisure Centre, St Mary Street.
◆ Swimming Pool - East Sands Leisure Centre (as above).

St Andrews Castle ruins

St Andrews 18th Green

STIRLING

Situated on the River Forth, Stirling 'The Gateway to the Highlands' has from Medieval times been strategically regarded as the most important place in Scotland. Through time, the centrality of its location ensured that whoever held Stirling controlled the nation and it is therefore inevitable that much of Scotland's history intrinsically revolves around the ancient capital. The 13th & 14th century Wars of Independence, Wallace's victory over the English at Stirling Bridge in 1297 when he outmanoeuvred the English by taking advantage of the river as a natural defence to divide the English army and force their retreat and numerous other battles were fought in close proximity to the Burgh. It was the victory at Stirling Bridge that inspired the fight for autonomy from English domination and though Wallace was later defeated at Falkirk in 1298, betrayed and brutally executed in London, his determination to free Scotland would live on. It was in 1314 that the reward came when King Robert the Bruce led his nation to freedom at the Battle of Bannockburn. An uneasy peace was born out of the 1314 victory and slowly the castle made the transition from fortification to Royal residence. Today, much of Stirling's heritage is still visible, the old town centering around Broad Street and St John's Street retains its charm with cobbled streets and numerous historic buildings. The National Wallace Monument stands to the north east of Stirling, overlooking the site of the Battle of Stirling Bridge. The Back Walk offers a scenic route through the town to Gowan Hill and during the summer months open top heritage bus tours operate which provide a fascinating insight into this historic town.

PLACES OF INTEREST

Visit Scotland Information Centre (All Year) - Old Town Jail, St John Street. FK8 1EA. Tel: (01786) 475019
Visit Scotland Information Point (All Year) - Customer First, 1-5 Port Street. FK8 2EJ. Tel: (01786) 404040.
◆ ARGYLL & SUTHERLAND HIGHLANDERS REGIMENTAL MUSEUM - Reflects history of the Regiment from 1794 to the present day. Displays include uniforms, paintings, a collection of medals dating from Waterloo and a realistic model of a World War I trench. Stirling Castle.
◆ ARGYLL'S LODGING - (Historic Scotland) Built in 1630, this renaissance mansion is regarded as Scotland's most impressive surviving building of its period. (closed for essential maintenance). Castle Wynd.
◆ BEHEADING STONE - This former execution site reflects a bygone era of gruesome capital punishment. Many important figures were slain at this site, amongst whom were Murdoch Stewart, regent of Scotland during the imprisonment of James I in England. Gowan Hill.
◆ COWANE'S HOSPITAL - Known also as Stirling Guildhall, the hospital was built between 1634 & 1649 by John Cowane to provide for the aged members of the Guild of Merchants. Outside is a statue of its founder. Coffe shop. St John Street.
◆ KING'S KNOT - (Historic Scotland) The remaining octagonal mound once formed part of a magnificent 17th century formal knot garden below the castle. King's Park.
◆ LADIES ROCK - Once a popular vantage point for the ladies of the court to watch the Royal Tournaments, the rock allows panoramic views across to the Trossachs and Ben Lomond. Valley Cemetery.
◆ MAR'S WARK - (Historic Scotland) Standing at the head of the town, this renaissance building was commissioned by the Earl of Mar in 1569 and would have been built using stone from the ruined Cambuskenneth Abbey. It was damaged by cannon fire during the 1740's and the shell is all that remains. Castle Wynd.
◆ STAR PYRAMID - Monument in memory of Martyrs seeking religious freedom. Castle Wynd.
◆ STIRLING CASTLE - (Historic Scotland) Perched 250 ft on a volcanic outcrop commanding a dominant position over the burgh, Stirling Castle considered by many to be the grandest of all Scottish castles both in location and architecture. Favoured royal residence of the Stuart Monarchs, it stands as the focal point of Stirling's turbulent history. Upper Castle Hill.
◆ STIRLING CHURCH OF THE HOLY RUDE - Church where coronation of James VI was conducted in 1567. St John Street.
◆ STIRLING MERCAT CROSS - The Mercat Cross in Broad Street was once the focal point of the town's trading activity. The unicorn figure on top of the cross is known locally as 'the puggy'. Broad Street.
◆ STIRLING OLD BRIDGE - (Historic Scotland) Dating from 1400, this bridge was once of strategic importance as the most southerly crossing point across the River.
◆ STIRLING SMITH ART GALLERY & MUSEUM - Award winning museum & gallery presents a diverse exhibition programme along with a permanent collection of fine art. Visit 'The Stirling Story' a history of the city from its origins to the present day. Dumbarton Road.

ENTERTAINMENT
◆ Cinemas - Forthside Way. Macrobert Arts Centre, University of Stirling (N of Stirling)
◆ Concerts - Albert Halls, Dumbarton Road.
◆ Theatres - Macrobert Arts Centre (as above). Tolbooth Theatre, Broad Street.

SPORT AND LEISURE
◆ Ice Rink - The Peak at Stirling Sports Village (E of Stirling).
◆ Parks & Gardens - Royal Gardens, Dumbarton Road. King's Park (Stirling Golf Club),Queens Road.
◆ Sports Centres - The Peak at Stirling Sports Village (as above).
◆ Swimming Pool - The Peak at Stirling Sports Village (as above).
◆ Ten Pin Bowling - AMF Bowling, Forth Street.

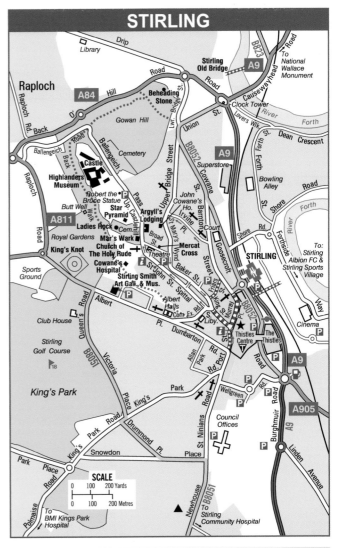

View from Stirling Castle

Stirling Castle

INDEX TO CITIES, TOWNS, VILLAGES, HAMLETS & LOCATIONS

(1) A strict alphabetical order is used e.g. Craig Lodge follows Craiglockhart but precedes Craigmalloch.

(2) The map reference given refers to the actual map square in which the town spot or built-up area is located and not to the place name.

(3) Where two or more places of the same name occur in the same County or Unitary Authority, the nearest large town is also given;
e.g. Achiemore. *High* . . . .2E **57** nr. Durness indicates that Achiemore is located in square 2E on page **57** and is situated near Durness in the Unitary Authority of Highland.

(4) Major towns are shown in bold, i.e. **Aberdeen**. *Aber* . . . . **69** (3E **43**). Where they appear on a Town Plan a second page reference is given.

COUNTIES AND UNITARY AUTHORITIES with the abbreviations used in this index

Aberdeen : *Aber*	Dumfries & Galloway : *Dum*	Edinburgh : *Edin*	Midlothian : *Midl*	Perth & Kinross : *Per*	South Lanarkshire : *S Lan*
Aberdeenshire : *Abers*	Dundee : *D'dee*	Falkirk : *Falk*	Moray : *Mor*	Renfrewshire : *Ren*	Stirling : *Stir*
Angus : *Ang*	East Ayrshire : *E Ayr*	Fife : *Fife*	North Ayrshire : *N Ayr*	Scottish Borders : *Bord*	West Dunbartonshire : *W Dun*
Argyll & Bute : *Arg*	East Dunbartonshire : *E Dun*	Glasgow : *Glas*	North Lanarkshire : *N Lan*	Shetland : *Shet*	Western Isles : *W Isl*
Clackmannanshire : *Clac*	East Lothian : *E Lot*	Highland : *High*	Northumberland : *Nmbd*	South Ayrshire : *S Ayr*	West Lothian : *W Lot*
Cumbria : *Cumb*	East Renfrewshire : *E Ren*	Inverclyde : *Inv*	Orkney : *Orkn*		

A

Abbey St Bathans *Bord* 2E **21**
Abbeytown *Cumb* 3E **7**
Aberarder *High* 1H **39**
Aberargie *Per* 2C **26**
Aberchalder *High* 3E **39**
Aberchirder *Abers* 3B **50**
Abercorn *W Lot* 1F **19**
Abercrombie *Fife* 3G **27**
Aberdalgie *Per* 1B **26**
Aberdeen *Aber* **69** (3E **43**)
Aberdeen International Airport *Aber* 2D **42**
Aberdour *Fife* 5C **26**
Aberfeldy *Per* 4D **32**
Aberfoyle *Stir* 3E **25**
Aberlady *E Lot* 5F **27**
Aberlemno *Ang* 3C **34**
Abernethy *Per* 2C **26**
Abernyte *Per* 5H **33**
Aberuthven *Per* 2A **26**
Abhainn Suidhe *W Isl* 4B **62**
Abington *S Lan* 1G **11**
Aboyne *Abers* 4A **42**
Abriachan *High* 5G **47**
Abronhill *N Lan* 1C **18**
Abune-the-Hill *Orkn* 2B **64**
Acairseid *W Isl* 4C **60**
Acha *Arg* 3C **28**
Achachork *High* 4D **44**
Achadh a' Chuirn *High* 1F **37**
Achahoish *Arg* 1A **16**
Achaleven *Arg* 5C **30**
Achallader *Arg* 4G **31**
Acha Mor *W Isl* 2E **62**
Achanalt *High* 2D **46**
Achandunie *High* 1H **47**
Ach' an Todhair *High* 1D **30**
Achany *High* 3C **54**
Achaphubuil *High* 1D **30**
Acharacle *High* 2H **29**
Acharn *Ang* 1H **33**
Acharn *Per* 4C **32**
Acharole *High* 3F **59**
Achateny *High* 2G **29**
Achavanich *High* 4E **59**
Achdalieu *High* 1D **30**
Achduart *High* 3F **53**
Achentoul *High* 5B **58**
Achfary *High* 5D **56**
Achfrish *High* 2C **54**
Achgarve *High* 4D **52**
Achiemore *High*
nr. Durness 2E **57**
Achiemore *High*
nr. Thurso 3B **58**
A' Chill *High* 3B **36**
Achiltibuie *High* 3E **53**
Achina *High* 2A **58**
Achinahuagh *High* 2G **57**
Achindarroch *High* 3D **30**
Achinduich *High* 3C **54**
Achinduin *Arg* 5B **30**
Achininver *High* 2G **57**
Achintee *High* 4A **46**
Achintraid *High* 5H **45**
Achleck *Arg* 4F **29**
Achlorachan *High* 3E **47**
Achluachrach *High* 5D **38**
Achlyness *High* 3D **56**
Achmelvich *High* 1F **53**
Achmony *High* 5G **47**
Achmore *High*
nr. Stromeferry 5H **45**
Achmore *High*
nr. Ullapool 4F **53**
Achnacarnin *High* 5B **56**
Achnacarry *High* 5C **38**
Achnaclerach *High* 2F **47**
Achnacloich *High* 3E **37**
Ach na Cloiche *High* 3E **37**
Achnaconeran *High* 2F **39**
Achnacroish *Arg* 4B **30**
Achnafalnich *Arg* 1B **24**
Achnagarron *High* 1H **47**
Achnagoul *Arg* 3H **23**
Achnaha *High* 2F **29**
Achnahanat *High* 4C **54**
Achnahannet *High* 1C **40**
Achnairn *High* 2C **54**
Achnamara *Arg* 5E **23**
Achnanellan *High* 5B **38**
Achnasheen *High* 3C **46**
Achnashellach *High* 4B **46**
Achosnich *High* 2F **29**
Achow *High* 5F **59**
Achranich *High* 4A **30**
Achreamie *High* 2D **58**
Achriabhach *High* 2E **31**
Achriesgill *High* 3D **56**
Achrimsdale *High* 3G **55**
Achscrabster *High* 2D **58**
Achtoty *High* 2H **57**
Achuvoldrach *High* 3G **57**
Achvaich *High* 4E **55**
Achvoan *High* 3E **55**
Ackergill *High* 3G **59**
Ackergillshore *High* 3G **59**
Adabroc *W Isl* 1K **63**
Addiewell *W Lot* 2E **19**
Addinston *Bord* 3C **20**
Advie *High* 5E **49**
Adziel *Abers* 3E **51**
Ae *Dum* 5G **11**
Affleck *Abers* 1D **42**
Affric Lodge *High* 1C **38**
Aglionby *Cumb* 3H **7**
Aiginis *W Isl* 4J **63**
Aikers *Orkn* 5D **64**
Aiketgate *Cumb* 4H **7**
Aikhead *Cumb* 4F **7**
Aikton *Cumb* 3F **7**
Aird *Arg* 3E **23**
Aird *Dum* 2B **4**
Aird *High*
nr. Port Henderson 1G **45**
Aird *High*
nr. Tarskavaig 3E **37**
The Aird *High* 3D **44**
Aird *W Isl*
on Benbecula 5H **61**
Aird *W Isl*
on Isle of Lewis 4K **63**
Àird a Bhasair *High* 3F **37**
Aird a Mhachair *W Isl* 6H **61**
Aird a Mhulaidh *W Isl* 3C **62**
Aird Asaig *W Isl* 4C **62**
Aird Dhail *W Isl* 1J **63**
Airdens *High* 4D **54**
Airdeny *Arg* 1G **23**
Aird Mhidhinis *W Isl* 4C **60**
Aird Mhighe *W Isl*
nr. Ceann a Bhaigh 5C **62**
Aird Mhighe *W Isl*
nr. Fionnsabhagh 6B **62**
Aird Mhor *W Isl*
on Barra 4C **60**
Aird Mhor *W Isl*
on South Uist 6J **61**
Airdrie *N Lan* 2C **18**
Aird Shleibhe *W Isl* 6C **62**
Aird Thunga *W Isl* 4J **63**
Aird Uig *W Isl* 1B **62**
Airidh a Bhruaich *W Isl* 3D **62**
Airies *Dum* 2A **4**
Airntully *Per* 5F **33**
Airor *High* 3G **37**
Airth *Falk* 5A **26**
Aisgernis *W Isl* 2C **60**
Aith *Shet*
on Fetlar 4K **67**
Aith *Shet*
on Mainland 1C **66**
Aithsetter *Shet* 3D **66**
Akeld *Nmbd* 5G **21**
Alcaig *High* 3G **47**
Aldclune *Per* 2E **33**
Aldochlay *Arg* 4C **24**
Aldoth *Cumb* 4E **7**
Alexandria *W Dun* 5C **24**
Alford *Abers* 2A **42**
Aline Lodge *W Isl* 3C **62**
Alladale Lodge *High* 5B **54**
Allanbank *N Lan* 3D **18**
Allanton *N Lan* 3D **18**
Allanton *Bord* 3F **21**
Allerby *Cumb* 5D **6**
Alligin Shuas *High* 3H **45**
Alloa *Clac* 4H **25**
Allonby *Cumb* 4D **6**
Alloway *S Ayr* 2A **10**
Alltgobhlach *N Ayr* 4B **16**
Alltnacaillich *High* 4F **57**
Allt na h' Airbhe *High* 4G **53**
Alltour *High* 5D **38**
Alltsigh *High* 2F **39**
Almondbank *Per* 1B **26**
Alness *High* 2H **47**
Alnessferry *High* 2H **47**
Altandhu *High* 2E **53**
Altanduin *High* 1F **55**
Altass *High* 3B **54**
Alterwall *High* 2F **59**
Altgaltraig *Arg* 1D **16**
Altnabreac *High* 4D **58**
Altnacealgach *High* 2H **53**
Altnafeadh *High* 3F **31**
Altnaharra *High* 5G **57**
Altonhill *E Ayr* 5H **17**
Altrua *High* 4D **38**
Alva *Clac* 4H **25**
Alves *Mor* 2E **49**
Alvie *High* 3B **40**
Alwinton *Nmbd* 3H **13**
Alyth *Per* 4H **33**
Amatnatua *High* 4B **54**
Am Baile *W Isl* 3C **60**
Amisfield *Dum* 5H **11**
Amulree *Per* 5E **33**
Anaheilt *High* 2B **30**
An Àird *High* 3E **37**
An Camus Darach
High 4F **37**
An Cnoc *W Isl* 4J **63**
An Cnoc Ard *W Isl* 1K **63**
An Coroghon *High* 3B **36**
Ancroft *Nmbd* 4H **21**
Ancrum *Bord* 1F **13**
Anderston *Glas* 7B **78**
An Dùnan *High* 1E **37**
Angerton *Cumb* 3F **7**
An Gleann Ur *W Isl* 4J **63**
Ankerville *High* 1B **48**
An Leth Meadhanach
W Isl 3C **60**
Annan *Dum* 2F **7**
Annat *Arg* 1H **23**
Annat *High* 3H **45**
Annathill *N Lan* 1C **18**
Annbank *S Ayr* 1B **10**
An Sailean *High* 2H **29**
Anston *S Lan* 4F **19**
Anstruther Easter *Fife* 3G **27**
Anstruther Wester *Fife* 3G **27**
An Taobh Tuath *W Isl* 2K **61**
An t-Aodann Ban *High* 3C **44**
An t Ath Leathann
High 1F **37**
An Teanga *High* 3F **37**
Anthorn *Cumb* 3E **7**
An t-Òb *W Isl* 6B **62**
An t-Òrd *High* 2F **37**
Anwoth *Dum* 3G **5**
Appin *Arg* 4C **30**
Applecross *High* 4G **45**
Applegarthtown *Dum* 5A **12**
Applethwaite *Cumb* 5F **7**
Appletreehall *Bord* 2E **13**
Arabella *High* 1B **48**
Arasaig *High* 5F **37**
Arbeadie *Abers* 4B **42**
Arbirlot *Ang* 4D **34**
Arbroath *Ang* 4D **34**
Arbuthnott *Abers* 1F **35**
Arcan *High* 3G **47**
Archargary *High* 3A **58**
Archiestown *Mor* 4F **49**
Ardachu *High* 3D **54**
Ardalanish *Arg* 2A **22**
Ardaneaskan *High* 5H **45**
Ardarroch *High* 5H **45**
Ardbeg *Arg*
nr. Dunoon 5A **24**
Ardbeg *Arg*
on Islay 4F **15**
Ardbeg *Arg*
on Isle of Bute 2D **16**
Ardcharnich *High* 5G **53**
Ardchiavaig *Arg* 2A **22**
Ardchonnell *Arg* 2G **23**
Ardchrishnish *Arg* 1B **22**
Ardchronie *High* 5D **54**
Ardchullarie *Stir* 2E **25**
Ardchyle *Stir* 1E **25**
Ard-dhubh *High* 4G **45**
Ardechive *High* 4C **38**
Ardelve *High* 1H **37**
Arden *Arg* 5C **24**
Ardendrain *High* 5G **47**
Ardentinny *Arg* 5A **24**
Ardeonaig *Stir* 5B **32**
Ardersier *High* 3A **48**
Ardery *High* 2A **30**
Ardessie *High* 5F **53**
Ardfern *Arg* 3F **23**
Ardfernal *Arg* 1G **15**
Ardfin *Arg* 2F **15**
Ardgartan *Arg* 3B **24**
Ardgay *High* 4D **54**
Ardgour *High* 2D **30**
Ardheslaig *High* 3G **45**
Ardindrean *High* 5G **53**
Ardlamont House
Arg 2C **16**
Ardler *Per* 4H **33**
Ardlui *Arg* 2C **24**
Ardlussa *Arg* 5D **22**
Ardmair *High* 4G **53**
Ardmay *Arg* 3B **24**
Ardminish *Arg* 4H **15**
Ardmolich *High* 1A **30**
Ardmore *High*
nr. Kinlochbervie 3D **56**
Ardmore *High*
nr. Tain 5E **55**
Ardnacross *Arg* 4G **29**
Ardnadam *Arg* 5A **24**
Ardnagrask *High* 4G **47**
Ardnamurach *High* 4H **37**
Ardnarff *High* 5H **45**
Ardnastang *High* 2B **30**
Ardoch *Per* 5F **33**
Ardochy House *High* 3D **38**
Ardpatrick *Arg* 2A **16**
Ardrishaig *Arg* 5F **23**
Ardroag *High* 4B **44**
Ardross *High* 1H **47**
Ardrossan *N Ayr* 4F **17**
Ardshealach *High* 2H **29**
Ardslignish *High* 2G **29**
Ardtalla *Arg* 3F **15**
Ardtalnaig *Per* 5C **32**
Ardtoe *High* 1H **29**
Arduaine *Arg* 2E **23**
Ardullie *High* 2G **47**
Ardvasar *High* 3F **37**
Ardvorlich *Per* 1F **25**
Ardwell *Dum* 4C **4**
Ardwell *Mor* 5G **49**
Arean *High* 1H **29**
Aridhglas *Arg* 1A **22**
Arinacrinachd *High* 3G **45**
Arinagour *Arg* 3D **28**
Arisaig *High* 5F **37**
Ariundle *High* 2B **30**
Arivegaig *High* 2H **29**
Armadail *High* 3F **37**
Armadale *High*
nr. Isleornsay 3F **37**
Armadale *High*
nr. Strathy 2A **58**
Armadale *W Lot* 2E **19**
Armathwaite *Cumb* 4H **7**
Arncroach *Fife* 3G **27**
Arnicle *Arg* 5A **16**
Arnisdale *High* 2H **37**
Arnish *High* 4E **45**
Arniston *Midl* 2A **20**
Arnol *W Isl* 3H **63**
Arnprior *Stir* 4F **25**
Aros Mains *Arg* 4G **29**
Arpafeelie *High* 3H **47**
Arrochar *Arg* 3B **24**
Arscaig *High* 2C **54**
Artafallie *High* 4H **47**
Arthrath *Abers* 5E **51**
Arthurstone *Per* 4H **33**
Ascog *Arg* 2E **17**
Ashfield *Stir* 3G **25**
Ashgill *S Lan* 4C **18**
Ashgrove *Mor* 2F **49**
Ashkirk *Bord* 1D **12**
Ashton *Inv* 1F **17**
Aspatria *Cumb* 4E **7**
Astle *High* 4E **55**
Athelstaneford *E Lot* 1C **20**
Ath-Tharracail *High* 2H **29**
Attadale *High* 5A **46**
Aucharnie *Abers* 4B **50**
Auchattie *Abers* 4B **42**
Auchavan *Ang* 2G **33**
Auchbreck *Mor* 1F **41**
Auchenback *E Ren* 3A **18**
Auchenblae *Abers* 1E **35**
Auchenbrack *Dum* 4E **11**
Auchenbreck *Arg* 5H **23**
Auchencairn *Dum*
nr. Dalbeattie 3A **6**
Auchencairn *Dum*
nr. Dumfries 5G **11**
Auchencarroch *W Dun* 5D **24**
Auchencrow *Bord* 2F **21**
Auchendennan *Arg* 5C **24**
Auchendinny *Midl* 2H **19**
Auchengray *S Lan* 3E **19**
Auchenhalrig *Mor* 2G **49**
Auchenheath *S Lan* 4D **18**
Auchenlochan *Arg* 1C **16**
Auchenmade *N Ayr* 4G **17**
Auchenmalg *Dum* 3D **4**
Auchentiber *N Ayr* 4G **17**
Auchenvennel *Arg* 5B **24**
Auchindrain *Arg* 3H **23**
Auchininna *Abers* 4B **50**
Auchinleck *Dum* 1F **5**
Auchinleck *E Ayr* 1C **10**
Auchinloch *N Lan* 1B **18**
Auchinstarry *N Lan* 1C **18**
Auchleven *Abers* 1B **42**
Auchlochan *S Lan* 5D **18**
Auchlunachan *High* 5G **53**
Auchmillan *E Ayr* 1C **10**
Auchmithie *Ang* 4D **34**
Auchmuirbridge *Fife* 3D **26**
Auchmull *Ang* 1C **34**
Auchnacree *Ang* 2B **34**
Auchnafree *Per* 5D **32**
Auchnagallin *High* 5D **48**
Auchnagatt *Abers* 4E **51**
Aucholzie *Abers* 4G **41**
Auchreddie *Abers* 4D **50**
Auchterarder *Per* 2A **26**
Auchteraw *High* 3E **39**
Auchterderran *Fife* 4D **26**
Auchterhouse *Ang* 5A **34**
Auchtermuchty *Fife* 2D **26**
Auchterneed *High* 3F **47**
Auchtertool *Fife* 4D **26**
Auchtertyre *High* 1H **37**
Auchtubh *Stir* 1E **25**
Auckengill *High* 2G **59**
Auds *Abers* 2B **50**
Aughertree *Cumb* 5F **7**
Auldearn *High* 3C **48**
Auldgirth *Dum* 5G **11**
Auldhouse *S Lan* 3B **18**
Ault a' chruinn *High* 1A **38**
Aultbea *High* 5D **52**
Aultdearg *High* 2D **46**
Aultgrishan *High* 5C **52**
Aultguish Inn *High* 1E **47**
Aultibea *High* 1H **55**
Aultiphurst *High* 2B **58**
Aultivullin *High* 2B **58**
Aultmore *Mor* 3H **49**
Aultnamain Inn *High* 5D **54**
Avielochan *High* 2C **40**
Aviemore *High* **70** (2B **40**)
Avoch *High* 3A **48**
Avonbridge *Falk* 1E **19**
Ayr *S Ayr* **70** (1A **10**)
Ayres of Selivoe *Shet* 2B **66**
Ayton *Bord* 2G **21**
Aywick *Shet* 4J **67**

B

Bac *W Isl* 3J **63**
Backaland *Orkn* 1E **64**
Backaskaill *Orkn* 2G **65**
Backfolds *Abers* 3F **51**
Backhill *Abers* 5C **50**
Backhill of Clackriach
Abers 4E **51**
Backies *High* 3F **55**
Backmuir of New Gilston
Fife 3F **27**
Back of Keppoch *High* 5F **37**
Badachonacher *High* 1H **47**
Badachro *High* 1G **45**
Badanloch Lodge *High* 5A **58**
Badavanich *High* 3C **46**
Badcall *High* 3D **56**
Badcaul *High* 4F **53**
Baddidarach *High* 1F **53**
Baddoch *Abers* 5E **41**
Badenscallie *High* 3F **53**
Badenscoth *Abers* 5C **50**
Badentarbat *High* 2F **53**
Badicaul *High* 1G **37**
Badlipster *High* 4F **59**
Badluarach *High* 4E **53**
Badnaban *High* 1F **53**
Badnabay *High* 4D **56**
Badnagie *High* 5E **59**
Badnellan *High* 3F **55**
Badninish *High* 4E **55**
Badrallach *High* 4F **53**
Bàgh a Chàise *W Isl* 3K **61**
Bàgh a' Chaisteil *W Isl* 5B **60**
Baghasdal *W Isl* 3C **60**
Bagh Mor *W Isl* 5J **61**
Bagh Shiarabhagh *W Isl* 4C **60**
Baile *W Isl* 2K **61**
Baile Ailein *W Isl* 2D **62**
Baile an Truiseil *W Isl* 2H **63**
Baile Boidheach *Arg* 1A **16**
Baile Glas *W Isl* 5J **61**
Bailemeonach *Arg* 4H **29**
Baile Mhanaich *W Isl* 5H **61**
Baile Mhartainn *W Isl* 3H **61**
Baile MhicPhail *W Isl* 3J **61**
Baile Mór *Arg* 1A **22**
Baile Mor *W Isl* 4H **61**
Baile nan Cailleach *W Isl* 5H **61**
Baile Raghaill *W Isl* 4H **61**
Baileyhead *Cumb* 5E **13**
Bailiesward *Abers* 5H **49**
Bail' Iochdrach *W Isl* 5J **61**
Baillieston *Glas* 2B **18**
Bail Uachdraich *W Isl* 4J **61**
Bail' Ur Tholastaidh *W Isl* 3K **63**
Bainsford *Falk* 5H **25**
Bainshole *Abers* 5B **50**
Baintown *Fife* 3E **27**
Balachuirn *High* 4E **45**
Balbeg *High*
nr. Cannich 5F **47**
Balbeg *High*
nr. Loch Ness 1F **39**
Balbeggie *Per* 1C **26**
Balblair *High*
nr. Bonar Bridge 4C **54**
Balblair *High*
nr. Invergordon 2A **48**
Balblair *High*
nr. Inverness 4G **47**
Balcathie *Ang* 5D **34**
Balchladich *High* 5B **56**
Balchraggan *High* 4G **47**
Balchrick *High* 3C **56**
Balcurvie *Fife* 3E **27**
Baldinnie *Fife* 2F **27**
Baldwinholme *Cumb* 3G **7**
Balearn *Abers* 3F **51**
Balemartine *Arg* 4A **28**
Balephetrish *Arg* 4B **28**
Balephuil *Arg* 4A **28**
Balerno *Edin* 2G **19**
Balevullin *Arg* 4A **28**
Balfield *Ang* 2C **34**
Balfour *Orkn* 3D **64**
Balfron *Stir* 5E **25**
Balgaveny *Abers* 4B **50**
Balgonar *Fife* 4B **26**
Balgowan *High* 4H **39**
Balgown *High* 2C **44**
Balgrochan *E Dun* 1B **18**
Balgy *High* 3H **45**
Balhalgardy *Abers* 1C **42**
Baliasta *Shet* 2K **67**
Baligill *High* 2B **58**
Balintore *Ang* 3H **33**
Balintore *High* 1B **48**
Balintraid *High* 1A **48**
Balkeerie *Ang* 4A **34**
Ballachulish *High* 3D **30**
Ballantrae *S Ayr* 5F **9**
Ballater *Abers* 4G **41**
Ballencrieff *E Lot* 1B **20**
Ballencrieff Toll *W Lot* 1E **19**
Ballentoul *Per* 2D **32**
Balliemore *Arg*
nr. Dunoon 5H **23**
Balliemore *Arg*
nr. Oban 1F **23**
Ballieward *High* 5D **48**
Ballimore *Stir* 2E **25**
Ballingry *Fife* 4C **26**
Ballinluig *Per* 3E **33**
Ballintuim *Per* 3G **33**
Balliveolan *Arg* 4B **30**
Balloan *High* 3C **54**
Balloch *High* 4A **48**
Balloch *N Lan* 1C **18**
Balloch *Per* 2H **25**
Balloch *W Dun* 5C **24**
Ballochan *Abers* 4A **42**
Ballochgoy *Arg* 2D **16**
Ballochmyle *E Ayr* 1C **10**
Ballochroy *Arg* 3A **16**
Ballygown *Arg* 4F **29**
Ballygrant *Arg* 2E **15**
Ballymichael *N Ayr* 5C **16**
Balmacara *High* 1H **37**
Balmaclellan *Dum* 1H **5**
Balmacqueen *High* 1D **44**
Balmaha *Stir* 4D **24**
Balmalcolm *Fife* 3E **27**
Balmalloch *N Lan* 1C **18**
Balmeanach *High* 5E **45**
Balmedie *Abers* 2E **43**
Balmerino *Fife* 1E **27**
Balmore *E Dun* 1B **18**
Balmore *High* 4B **44**
Balmullo *Fife* 1F **27**
Balmurrie *Dum* 2D **4**
Balnaboth *Ang* 2A **34**
Balnabruaich *High* 1A **48**
Balnabruich *High* 5E **59**
Balnacoil *High* 2F **55**
Balnacra *High* 4A **46**
Balnacroft *Abers* 4F **41**
Balnageith *Mor* 3D **48**
Balnaglaic *High* 5F **47**
Balnagrantach *High* 5F **47**
Balnaguard *Per* 3E **33**
Balnahard *Arg* 4B **22**
Balnain *High* 5F **47**
Balnakeil *High* 2E **57**
Balnaknock *High* 2D **44**
Balnamoon *Abers* 3E **51**
Balnamoon *Ang* 2C **34**
Balnapaling *High* 2B **48**
Balornock *Glas* 2B **18**
Balquhidder *Stir* 1E **25**
Baltasound *Shet* 2K **67**
Baltersan *Dum* 2F **5**
Balthangie *Abers* 3D **50**
Balvaird *High* 3G **47**
Balvaird *Per* 2C **26**
Balvenie *Mor* 4G **49**
Balvicar *Arg* 2E **23**
Balvraid *High* 2H **37**
Balvraid Lodge *High* 5B **48**
Banavie *High* 1E **31**
Banchory *Abers* 4B **42**
Banchory-Devenick *Abers* 3E **43**
Banff *Abers* 2B **50**
Bankend *Dum* 2D **6**
Bankfoot *Per* 5F **33**
Bankglen *E Ayr* 2D **10**
Bankhead *Aber* 2D **42**
Bankhead *Abers* 3B **42**
Bankhead *S Lan* 4D **18**
Banknock *Falk* 1C **18**
Bankshill *Dum* 5A **12**
Banniskirk *High* 3E **59**
Bannockburn *Stir* 4H **25**
Banton *N Lan* 1C **18**
Barabhas *W Isl* 2H **63**
Barabhas Iarach *W Isl* 3H **63**
Baramore *High* 1H **29**
Barassie *S Ayr* 5G **17**
Baravullin *Arg* 4C **30**
Barbaraville *High* 1A **48**
Barbhas Uarach *W Isl* 2H **63**
Barbieston *S Ayr* 2B **10**
Barcaldine *Arg* 4C **30**
Barclose *Cumb* 2H **7**
Bardister *Shet* 5G **67**
Bardnabeinne *High* 4E **55**
Bardowie *E Dun* 1A **18**
Bardrainney *Inv* 1G **17**
Barelees *Nmbd* 5F **21**
Bargeddie *N Lan* 2B **18**
Bargrennan *Dum* 1E **5**
Barharrow *Dum* 3H **5**
Barlanark *Glas* 2B **18**
Barmoor *Nmbd* 5H **21**
Barmulloch *Glas* 2B **18**
Barnbarroch *Dum* 3B **6**
Barnhead *Ang* 3D **34**
Barnhill *D'dee* 5B **34**
Barnhill *Mor* 3E **49**
Barnhill *Per* 1C **26**
Barnhills *Dum* 1A **4**
The Barony *Orkn* 2B **64**
Barr *Dum* 3E **11**
Barr *S Ayr* 4H **9**
Barra Airport *W Isl* 4B **60**
Barrachan *Dum* 4E **5**
Barraglom *W Isl* 1C **62**

Barrahormid—Ceann a Bhaigh

Barrahormid Arg 5E 23
Barrapol Arg 4A 28
Barravullin Arg 3F 23
Barrhead E Ren 3A 18
Barrhill S Ayr 5H 9
Barrmill N Ayr 3G 17
Barrock High 1F 59
Barrowburn Nmbd 2H 13
Barry Ang 5C 34
Barthol Chapel Abers 5D 50
Barton Cumb 5H 7
Bassendean Bord 4D 20
Bassenthwaite Cumb 5F 7
Basta Shet 3J 67
Bathgate W Lot 2E 19
Bathville W Lot 2E 19
Bauds of Cullen Mor 2H 49
Baugh Arg 4B 28
Bay High 3B 44
Beacrabhaic W Isl 5C 62
Beal Nmbd 4H 21
Beaquoy Orkn 2C 64
Bearsden E Dun 1A 18
Beattock Dum 3H 11
Beauly High 4G 47
Beaumont Cumb 3G 7
Beckfoot Cumb 4D 6
Bedrule Bord 2F 13
Beeswing Dum 2B 6
Beinn Casgro W Isl 5J 63
Beith N Ayr 3G 17
Belfatton Abers 3F 51
Belford Nmbd 5H 21
Belhaven E Lot 1D 20
Belhelvie Abers 2E 43
Belhinnie Abers 1H 41
Bellabeg Abers 2G 41
Belladrum High 4G 47
Bellamore S Ayr 5H 9
Bellanoch Arg 4F 23
Belleheiglash Mor 5E 49
Belle Vue Cumb 5E 7
Bellfield S Lan 5D 18
Belliehill Ang 2C 34
Bellingham Nmbd 5H 13
Bellochantuy Arg 5H 15
Bellsbank E Ayr 3B 10
Bellside N Lan 3D 18
Bellspool Bord 5G 19
Bellsquarry W Lot 2F 19
Belmaduthy High 3H 47
Belmont Shet 2J 67
Belmont S Ayr 1A 10
Belnacraig Abers 2G 41
Belston S Ayr 1A 10
Belts of Collonach Abers 4B 42
Bemersyde Bord 5C 20
Ben Alder Lodge High 1A 32
Ben Armine Lodge High 2E 55
Benbecula Airport W Isl 5H 61
Benbuie Dum 4E 11
Benderloch Arg 5C 30
Bendronaig Lodge High 5B 46
Benholm Abers 2F 35
Benmore Lodge High 2A 54
Bennecarrigan N Ayr 1E 9
Benston Shet 1D 66
Benstonhall Orkn 1E 64
Bent Abers 1D 34
Bentpath Dum 4C 12
Bents W Lot 2E 19
Benvie D'dee 5A 34
Beoraidbeg High 4F 37
Bernera High 1H 37
Bernice Arg 4A 24
Bernisdale High 3D 44
Berriedale High 1H 55
Berrier Cumb 5G 7
Berrington Nmbd 4H 21
Berrington Law Nmbd 4G 21
Berryhillock Mor 2A 50
Berryscaur Dum 4A 12
Berwick-upon-Tweed
Nmbd 3G 21
Bettyhill High 2A 58
Beul an Atha Arg 2E 15
Bewaldeth Cumb 5F 7
Bhalton W Isl 1B 62
Bhatarsaigh W Isl 5B 60
Bieldside Aber 3D 42
Biggar S Lan 5F 19
Biggings Shet 1A 66
Bighouse High 2B 58
Biglands Cumb 3F 7
Big Sand High 1G 45
Bigton Shet 4C 66
Bilbster High 3F 59
Bilston Midl 2H 19
Bimbister Orkn 3C 64
Bindal High 5G 55
Binniehill Falk 1D 18
Birchburn N Ayr 1E 9
Birchview Mor 5E 49
Birdston E Dun 1B 18
Birgham Bord 5E 21
Birichen High 4E 55
Birkby Cumb 5D 6
Birkenhills Abers 4C 50
Birkenshaw N Lan 2B 18
Birkhall Abers 4G 41
Birkhill Ang 5A 34
Birnam Per 4F 33
Birse Abers 4A 42
Birsemore Abers 4A 42
Birtley Nmbd 5H 13
Bishopbriggs E Dun 1B 18
Bishopmill Mor 2F 49
Bishopton Dum 4F 5
Bishopton Ren 1H 17
Bixter Shet 1C 66
Blackburn Abers 2D 42
Blackburn W Lot 2E 19
Black Clauchrie S Ayr 5H 9
Black Corries High 3F 31
Black Crofts Arg 5C 30
Blackdog Abers 2E 43
Blackdyke Cumb 3E 7
Blackford Cumb 2G 7
Blackford Per 3H 25
Blackhall Edin 1H 19
Blackhall Ren 2H 17
Blackhill Abers 4F 51
Blackhill High 3C 44
Blackhills Abers 2E 51
Blackhills High 3C 48
Blacklunans Per 2G 33
Black Mount Arg 4F 31
Blackness Falk 1F 19
Blackpool Gate Cumb 5E 13
Blackridge W Lot 2D 18
Blackrock Arg 2E 15
Blackshaw Dum 2D 6
Blacktop Aber 3D 42
Blackwaterfoot N Ayr 1D 8
Blackwood Dum 5G 11
Blackwood S Lan 4C 18
Bladnoch Dum 3F 5
Blaich High 1D 30
Blain High 2H 29
Blair Atholl Per 2D 32
Blair Drummond Stir 4G 25
Blairgowrie Per 4G 33
Blairhall Fife 5B 26
Blairingone Per 4A 26
Blairlogie Stir 4H 25
Blairmore Abers 5H 49
Blairmore Arg 5A 24
Blairmore High 3C 56
Blairquhanan W Dun 5D 24
Blandy High 2H 57
Blanefield Stir 1A 18
Blantyre S Lan 3B 18
Blarmachfoldach High 2D 30
Blarnalearoch High 4G 53
Blathaisbhal W Isl 3J 61
Blebocraigs Fife 2F 27
Blencogo Cumb 4E 7
Blennerhasset Cumb 4E 7
Blindburn Nmbd 2H 13
Blindcrake Cumb 5E 7
Blitterlees Cumb 3E 7
Bloomfield Bord 1E 13
Blyth Bord 4G 19
Blyth Bank Bord 4G 19
Blyth Bridge Bord 4G 19
Boarhills Fife 2G 27
Boath High 1G 47
Boat of Garten High 2C 40
Boddam Abers 4G 51
Boddam Shet 5C 66
Bogallan High 3H 47
Bogbrae Croft Abers 5F 51
Bogend S Ayr 5G 17
Boghall Midl 2H 19
Boghall W Lot 2E 19
Boghead S Lan 4C 18
Bogindollo Ang 3B 34
Bogmoor Mor 2G 49
Bogniebrae Abers 4A 50
Bograxie Abers 2C 42
Bogside N Lan 3D 18
Bogton Abers 3B 50
Bogue Dum 5D 10
Bohenie High 5D 38
Boirseam W Isl 6B 62
Boleside Bord 5B 20
Bolshan Ang 3D 34
Boltachan Per 3D 32
Bolton E Lot 1C 20
Boltonfellend Cumb 2H 7
Boltongate Cumb 4F 7
Bolton Low Houses Cumb 4F 7
Bolton New Houses Cumb 4F 7
Bolton Wood Lane Cumb 4F 7
Bonar Bridge High 4D 54
Bonawe Arg 5D 30
Bonchester Bridge Bord 2E 13
Bo'ness Falk 5A 26
Bonhill W Dun 1G 17
Bonjedward Bord 1F 13
Bonkle N Lan 3D 18
Bonnington Ang 5C 34
Bonnington Edin 2G 19
Bonnybank Fife 3E 27
Bonnybridge Falk 5H 25
Bonnykelly Abers 3D 50
Bonnyrigg Midl 2A 20
Bonnyton Ang 5A 34
Bonnytown Fife 2G 27
Booth of Toft Shet 5H 67
Boquhan Stir 5E 25
Bordlands Bord 4G 19
Boreland Dum 4A 12
Borestone Brae Stir 4G 25
Borgh W Isl
on Barra 4B 60
Borgh W Isl
on Benbecula 5H 61
Borgh W Isl
on Berneray 2K 61
Borgh W Isl
on Isle of Lewis 2J 63
Borghasdal W Isl 6B 62
Borghastan W Isl 3F 63
Borgh na Sgiotaig High 1C 44
Borgie High 3H 57
Borgue Dum 4H 5
Borgue High 5E 59
Borlum High 1G 39
Bornais W Isl 2C 60
Bornesketaig High 1C 44
Borreraig High 3A 44
Borrobol Lodge High 1F 55
Borrodale High 4A 44
Borrowston High 4G 59
Borrowstonehill Orkn 4D 64
Borrowstoun Falk 5A 26
Borthwick Midl 3A 20
Borve High 4D 44
Bostadh W Isl 3F 63
Bothel Cumb 5E 7
Bothwell S Lan 3C 18
Bottacks High 2F 47
Bottomcraig Fife 1E 27
Bousd Arg 2D 28
Bousta Shet 1B 66
Boustead Hill Cumb 3F 7
Bowden Bord 5C 20
Bower Nmbd 5G 13
Bowermadden High 2F 59
Bowershall Fife 4B 26
Bowertower High 2F 59
Bowhousebog N Lan 3D 18
Bowling W Dun 1H 17
Bowmore Arg 3E 15
Bowness-on-Solway Cumb 2F 7
Bow of Fife Fife 2E 27
Bowriefauld Ang 4C 34
Bowscale Cumb 5G 7
Bowsden Nmbd 4G 21
Bowside Lodge High 2B 58
Boyndie Abers 2B 50
Braal Castle High 3E 59
Brabster High 2G 59
Bracadale High 5C 44
Bracara High 4G 37
Brackenlands Cumb 4F 7
Brackenthwaite Cumb 4F 7
Brackla High 3B 48
Brackletter High 5C 38
Brackloch High 1G 53
Braco Per 3H 25
Bracobrae Mor 3A 50
Brae High 5D 52
Brae Shet 6G 67
Braeantra High 1G 47
Braefield High 5F 47
Braefindon High 3H 47
Braegrum Per 1B 26
Braehead Ang 3D 34
Braehead Dum 3F 5
Braehead Mor 4F 49
Braehead Orkn 3G 65
Braehead S Lan
nr. Coalburn 5D 18
Braehead S Lan
nr. Forth 3E 19
Braehoulland Shet 5F 67
Braemar Abers 4E 41
Braemore High
nr. Dunbeath 5D 58
Braemore High
nr. Ullapool 1C 46
Brae of Achnahaird High 2F 53
Brae Roy Lodge High 4E 39
Braeside Abers 5E 51
Braeside Inv 1F 17
Braes of Coul Ang 3H 33
Braeswick Orkn 4J 65
Braetongue High 3G 57
Braeval Stir 3E 25
Braevallich Arg 3G 23
Braewick Shet 1C 66
Bragar W Isl 3G 63
Bragleenbeg Arg 1G 23
Braidwood S Lan 4D 18
Braigo Arg 2D 14
Brampton Cumb 2H 7
Branault High 2G 29
Branchill Mor 3D 48
Branderburgh Mor 1F 49
Branthwaite Cumb 5F 7
Branxholme Bord 2D 12
Branxton Nmbd 5F 21
Brathens Abers 4B 42
Braulen Lodge High 5D 46
Brawl High 2B 58
Brawlbin High 3D 58
Breacleit W Isl 1C 62
Breakachy High 4F 47
Breakish High 1F 37
Breanais W Isl 2A 62
Breascleit W Isl 1D 62
Brecais Àrd High 1F 37
Brecais Iosal High 1F 37
Brechin Ang 3D 34
Breibhig W Isl
on Barra 5B 60
Breibhig W Isl
on Isle of Lewis 4J 63
Breich W Lot 2E 19
Breiwick Shet 2D 66
Brenachie High 1A 48
Brettabister Shet 1D 66
Brewlands Bridge Ang 2G 33
Bridekirk Cumb 5E 7
Brideswell Abers 5A 50
Bridge End Cumb 4G 7
Bridge End Shet 3C 66
Bridgefoot Ang 5A 34
Bridgefoot Cumb 5D 6
Bridgend Abers
nr. Huntly 5A 50
Bridgend Abers
nr. Peterhead 5F 51
Bridgend Ang
nr. Brechin 2C 34
Bridgend Ang
nr. Kirriemuir 4A 34
Bridgend Arg
nr. Lochgilphead 4F 23
Bridgend Arg
on Islay 2E 15
Bridgend Fife 2E 27
Bridgend High 3E 47
Bridgend Mor 5G 49
Bridgend Per 1C 26
Bridgend W Lot 1F 19
Bridgend of Lintrathen
Ang 3H 33
Bridgeness Falk 5B 26
Bridge of Alford Abers 2A 42
Bridge of Allan Stir 4G 25
Bridge of Avon Mor 5E 49
Bridge of Awe Arg 1H 23
Bridge of Balgie Per 4A 32
Bridge of Brown High 1E 41
Bridge of Cally Per 3G 33
Bridge of Canny Abers 4B 42
Bridge of Dee Dum 2A 6
Bridge of Don Aber 2E 43
Bridge of Dun Ang 3D 34
Bridge of Dye Abers 5B 42
Bridge of Earn Per 2C 26
Bridge of Ericht Per 3A 32
Bridge of Feugh Abers 4C 42
Bridge of Gairn Abers 4G 41
Bridge of Gaur Per 3A 32
Bridge of Muchalls Abers 4D 42
Bridge of Oich High 3E 39
Bridge of Orchy Arg 5G 31
Bridge of Walls Shet 1B 66
Bridge of Weir Ren 2G 17
Brigham Cumb 5D 6
Brightons Falk 1E 19
Brig o' Turk Stir 3E 25
Brims Orkn 6B 64
Brindister Shet
nr. West Burrafirth 1B 66
Brindister Shet
nr. West Lerwick 3D 66
Brinian Orkn 2D 64
Brisco Cumb 3H 7
Broadfield Inv 1G 17
Broadford High 1F 37
Broadhaven High 3G 59
Broadley Mor 2G 49
Broadrashes Mor 3H 49
Broadsea Abers 2E 51
Broadwath Cumb 3H 7
Broallan High 4F 47
Brochel High 4E 45
Brocketsbrae S Lan 5D 18
Brockhill Bord 1C 12
Brockleymoor Cumb 5H 7
Brodick N Ayr 5D 16
Brodie Mor 3C 48
Brodiesord Abers 3A 50
Brogaig High 2D 44
Bromfield Cumb 4E 7
Brookfield Ren 2H 17
Broom Fife 3E 27
Broomend Abers 2C 42
Broomfield Abers 5E 51
Broomhill High
nr. Grantown-on-Spey 1C 40
Broomhill High
nr. Invergordon 1A 48
Broomhillbank Dum 4A 12
Broomlands Dum 3H 11
Broom of Moy Mor 3D 48
Brora High 3G 55
Broubster High 2D 58
Brough High 1F 59
Brough Orkn
nr. Finstown 3C 64
Brough Orkn
nr. St Margaret's Hope 6D 64
Brough Shet
nr. Benston 1D 66
Brough Shet
nr. Booth of Toft 5H 67
Brough Shet
on Bressay 2E 66
Brough Shet
on Whalsay 6J 67
Brough Lodge Shet 3J 67
Broughton Orkn 3G 65
Broughton Bord 5G 19
Broughton Cross Cumb 5D 6
Broughton Moor Cumb 5D 6
Broughtown Orkn 3J 65
Broughty Ferry D'dee 5B 34
Browland Shet 1B 66
Broxburn E Lot 1D 20
Broxburn W Lot 1F 19
Brù W Isl 3H 63
Bruach Mairi W Isl 4J 63
Bruairnis W Isl 4C 60
Bruan High 5G 59
Bruar Lodge Per 1D 32
Brucehill W Dun 1G 17
Brucklay Abers 3E 51
Bruichladdich Arg 2D 14
Brunery High 1A 30
Brunton Fife 1E 27
Brusta W Isl 2K 61
Brydekirk Dum 1E 7
Buaile nam Bodach W Isl 4C 60
Bualintur High 1D 36
Buccleuch Bord 2C 12
Buchanan Smithy Stir 5D 24
Buchanhaven Abers 4G 51
Buchanty Per 1A 26
Buchany Stir 3G 25
Buchley E Dun 1A 18
Buchlyvie Stir 4E 25
Buckabank Cumb 4G 7
Buckhaven Fife 4E 27
Buckholm Bord 5B 20
Buckie Mor 2H 49
Buckpool Mor 2H 49
Bucksburn Aber 3D 42
Buckton Nmbd 5H 21
Buldoo High 2C 58
Bullgill Cumb 5D 6
Bullwood Arg 1E 17
Bulwark Abers 4E 51
Bun Abhainn Eadarra W Isl 4C 62
Bunacaimb High 5F 37
Bun a' Mhuillinn W Isl 3C 60
Bunarkaig High 5C 38
Bunchrew High 4H 47
Bundalloch High 1H 37
Buness Shet 2K 67
Bunessan Arg 1A 22
Bunkegivie High 2G 39
Bunloit High 1G 39
Bunnahabhain Arg 1F 15
Bunoich High 3E 39
Bunree High 2D 30
Bunroy High 5D 38
Buntait High 5F 47
Burg Arg 4E 29
Burgh by Sands Cumb 3G 7
Burghead Mor 2E 49
Burgh Muir Abers 2C 42
Burland Shet 3C 66
Burness Orkn 3J 65
Burnfoot E Ayr 3B 10
Burnfoot Per 3A 26
Burnfoot Bord
nr. Hawick 2E 13
Burnfoot Bord
nr. Roberton 2D 12
Burnhaven Abers 4G 51
Burnhead Dum 4F 11
Burnhervie Abers 2C 42
Burnhouse N Ayr 3G 17
Burnmouth Bord 2G 21
Burn of Cambus Stir 3G 25
Burnside Ang 3C 34
Burnside E Ayr 2C 10
Burnside Per 3C 26
Burnside Shet 5E 67
Burnside S Lan 3B 18
Burnside W Lot
nr. Broxburn 1F 19
Burnside W Lot
nr. Winchburgh 1F 19
Burntisland Fife 5D 26
Burnton E Ayr 3B 10
Burnwynd Edin 2G 19
Burrafirth Shet 1K 67
Burragarth Shet 2J 67
Burravoe Shet
nr. North Roe 4G 67
Burravoe Shet
on Mainland 6G 67
Burravoe Shet
on Yell 5J 67
Burray Village Orkn 5D 64
Burrelton Per 5G 33
Burrigill High 5F 59
Burroughston Orkn 2E 64
Burthwaite Cumb 4H 7
Burwick Orkn 6D 64
Busby E Ren 3A 18
Busby Per 1B 26
Busta Shet 6G 67
Butterstone Per 4F 33
Butteryhaugh Nmbd 4F 13
Byrness Nmbd 3G 13

C

Cabharstadh W Isl 3E 62
Cabrach Arg 2F 15
Cabrach Mor 1G 41
Cadder E Dun 1B 18
Caddonfoot Bord 5B 20
Cadham Fife 3D 26
Caerlaverock Per 2H 25
Cairinis W Isl 4J 61
Cairisiadar W Isl 1B 62
Cairminis W Isl 6B 62
Cairnbaan Arg 4F 23
Cairnbulg Abers 2F 51
Cairncross Ang 1B 34
Cairndow Arg 2A 24
Cairness Abers 2F 51
Cairneyhill Fife 5B 26
Cairngarroch Dum 4B 4
Cairnhill Abers 5B 50
Cairnie Abers 4H 49
Cairnorrie Abers 4D 50
Cairnryan Dum 2B 4
Cairston Orkn 3B 64
Calanais W Isl 1D 62
Calbost W Isl 6J 63
Caldback Shet 2K 67
Caldbeck Cumb 5G 7
Calderbank N Lan 2C 18
Caldercruix N Lan 2D 18
Calder Mains High 3D 58
Caldermill S Lan 4B 18
Calderwood S Lan 3B 18
Calebrack Cumb 5G 7
Calfsound Orkn 1E 64
Calgary Arg 3E 29
Califer Mor 3D 48
California Falk 1E 19
Callakille High 3F 45
Callander Stir 3F 25
Callendoun Arg 5C 24
Calligarry High 3F 37
Calthwaite Cumb 4H 7
Calton Edin 3K 75
Calton Glas 8M 79
Calvine Per 2D 32
Calvo Cumb 3E 7
Camaghael High 1E 31
Camas-luinie High 1A 38
Camasnacroise High 3B 30
Camastianavaig High 5E 45
Camasunary High 2E 37
Camault Muir High 4G 47
Camb Shet 3J 67
Cambus Clac 4H 25
Cambusbarron Stir 4G 25
Cambuskenneth Stir 4H 25
Cambuslang S Lan 2B 18
Cambusnethan N Lan 3D 18
Cambus o' May Abers 4H 41
Camelon Falk 5H 25
Camerton Cumb 5D 6
Camghouran Per 3A 32
Cammachmore Abers 4E 43
Camore High 4E 55
Campbelton N Ayr 3E 17
Campbeltown Arg 1C 8
Campbeltown Airport Arg 1B 8
Cample Dum 4F 11
Campmuir Per 5H 33
Camptoun E Lot 1C 20
Camptown Bord 2F 13
Camserney Per 4D 32
Camster High 4F 59
Camus Croise High 2F 37
Camuscross High 2F 37
Camusdarach High 4F 37
Camusnagaul High
nr. Fort William 1D 30
Camusnagaul High
nr. Little Loch Broom 5F 53
Camusteel High 4G 45
Camusterrach High 4G 45
Camusvrachan Per 4B 32
Candy Mill S Lan 4F 19
Canisbay High 1G 59
Cannich High 5E 47
Canonbie Dum 1G 7
Canongate Edin 4J 75
Cantray High 4A 48
Cantraybruich High 4A 48
Cantraywood High 4A 48
Cantsdam Fife 4C 26
Caol High 1E 31
Caolas Arg 4B 28
Caolas W Isl 5B 60
Caolas Liubharsaigh W Isl 6J 61
Caolas Scalpaigh W Isl 5D 62
Caolas Stocinis W Isl 5C 62
Caol Ila Arg 1F 15
Caol Loch Ailse High 1G 37
Caol Reatha High 1G 37
Cappercleuch Bord 1B 12
Capplegill Dum 3A 12
Caputh Per 5F 33
Carbost High
nr. Loch Harport 5C 44
Carbost High
nr. Portree 4D 44
Carcluie S Ayr 2A 10
Cardenden Fife 4D 26
Cardewlees Cumb 3G 7
Cardno Abers 2E 51
Cardow Mor 4E 49
Cardross Arg 1G 17
Cardurnock Cumb 3E 7
Careston Ang 2C 34
Carfin N Lan 3C 18
Carfrae Bord 3C 20
Cargenbridge Dum 1C 6
Cargill Per 5G 33
Cargo Cumb 3G 7
Carham Nmbd 5F 21
Carie Per
nr. Loch Rannah 3B 32
Carie Per
nr. Loch Tay 5B 32
Carlabhagh W Isl 3G 63
Carleton Cumb 3H 7
Carlisle Cumb 3H 7
Carloonan Arg 2H 23
Carlops Bord 3G 19
Carluke S Lan 3D 18
Carmichael S Lan 5E 19
Carmunnock Glas 3B 18
Carmyle Glas 2B 18
Carmyllie Ang 4C 34
Carnach High
nr. Lochcarron 1B 38
Carnach High
nr. Ullapool 4F 53
Carnach Mor 4D 48
Carnach W Isl 5D 62
Carnachy High 3A 58
Carnain Arg 2E 15
Carnais W Isl 1B 62
Carnan Arg 4B 28
Carnan W Isl 6H 61
Carnbee Fife 3G 27
Carnbo Per 3B 26
Carndu High 1H 37
Carnell S Ayr 5H 17
Carn-gorm High 1A 38
Carnie Abers 3D 42
Carnock Fife 5B 26
Carnoustie Ang 5C 34
Carntyne Glas 2B 18
Carnwath S Lan 4E 19
Carradale Arg 5B 16
Carragraich W Isl 5C 62
Carrbridge High 1C 40
Carrick Castle Arg 4A 24
Carrick Ho Orkn 1E 64
Carriden Falk 5B 26
Carrington Midl 2A 20
Carron Falk 5H 25
Carron Mor 4F 49
Carronbridge Dum 4F 11
Carronshore Falk 5H 25
Carrutherstown Dum 1E 7
Carsaig Arg 1C 22
Carscreugh Dum 2D 4
Carsegowan Dum 3F 5
Carse House Arg 2A 16
Carseriggan Dum 2E 5
Carsethorn Dum 3C 6
Carskiey Arg 3B 8
Carsluith Dum 3F 5
Carsphairn Dum 4C 10
Carstairs S Lan 4E 19
Carstairs Junction S Lan 4E 19
Carterhaugh Ang 4B 34
Cartland S Lan 4D 18
Carwath Cumb 4G 7
Carwinley Cumb 1H 7
Cash Feus Fife 3D 26
Cashlie Per 4H 31
Castlebay W Isl 5B 60
Castlecary N Lan 1C 18
Castlecraig High 2B 48
Castle Douglas Dum 2A 6
Castle Heaton Nmbd 4G 21
Castlehill Per 5H 33
Castlehill S Lan 3D 18
Castlehill W Dun 1G 17
Castle Kennedy Dum 3C 4
Castle Lachlan Arg 4H 23
Castlemilk Glas 3B 18
Castle O'er Dum 4B 12
Castleton Abers 4E 41
Castleton Arg 5F 23
Castleton Mor 1E 41
Castleton Per 2A 26
Castletown Cumb 5H 7
Castletown High 2E 59
Catacol N Ayr 4C 16
Catcleugh Nmbd 3G 13
Catfirth Shet 1D 66
Cathcart Glas 2A 18
Catlodge High 4H 39
Catlowdy Cumb 1H 7
Catrine E Ayr 1C 10
Catterlen Cumb 5H 7
Catterline Abers 1F 35
Cauldhame Stir 4F 25
Cauldmill Bord 2E 13
Cauldwells Abers 3C 50
Caulkerbush Dum 3C 6
Caulside Dum 5D 12
Causewayend S Lan 5F 19
Causewayhead Stir 4H 25
Cawdor High 3B 48
Ceallan W Isl 5J 61
Ceann a Bhaigh W Isl
on North Uist 4H 61

Drumfearn—Gord

Drumfearn High 2F 37
Drumgask High 4H 39
Drumgelloch N Lan 2C 18
Drumgley Ang 3B 34
Drumguish High 4A 40
Drumin Mor 5E 49
Drumindorsair High 4F 47
Drumlamford House
S Ayr 1D 4
Drumlasie Abers 3B 42
Drumlemble Arg 2B 8
Drumlithie Abers 5C 42
Drummoddie Dum 4E 5
Drummond High 2H 47
Drummore Dum 5C 4
Drummuir Mor 4G 49
Drumnadrochit High 5G 47
Drumnagorrach Mor 3A 50
Drumoak Abers 4C 42
Drumrunie High 3G 53
Drumry W Dun 1A 18
Drums Abers 1E 43
Drumsleet Dum 1C 6
Drumsmittal High 4H 47
Drums of Park Abers 3A 50
Drumsturdy Ang 5B 34
Drumtochty Castle
Abers 5B 42
Drumuie High 4D 44
Drumuillie High 1C 40
Drumvaich Stir 3F 25
Drumwhindle Abers 5E 51
Drunkendub Ang 4D 34
Drybridge Mor 2H 49
Drybridge N Ayr 5G 17
Dryburgh Bord 5C 20
Drymen Stir 5D 24
Drymuir Abers 4E 51
Drynachan Lodge
High 5B 48
Drynie Park High 3G 47
Drynoch High 5D 44
Dubford Abers 2C 50
Dubiton Abers 3B 50
Dubton Ang 3C 34
Duchally High 2A 54
Duddingston Edin 1H 19
Duddo Nmbd 4G 21
Dufftown Mor 4G 49
Duffus Mor 2E 49
Duirinish High 5G 45
Duisdalemore High 2F 37
Duisdeil Mòr High 2F 37
Duisky High 1D 30
Dull Per 4D 32
Dullatur N Lan 1C 18
Dulnain Bridge High 1C 40
Dumbarton W Dun 1H 17
Dumfin Arg 5C 24
Dumfries Dum 71 (1C 6)
Dumgoyne Stir 5E 25
Dun Ang 2D 34
Dunagoil Arg 3D 16
Dunalastair Per 3C 32
Dunan High 1E 37
Dunbar E Lot 1D 20
Dunbeath High 5E 59
Dunbeg Arg 5B 30
Dunblane Stir 3G 25
Dunbog Fife 2D 26
Duncanston Abers 1A 42
Duncanston High 3G 47
Dun Charlabhaigh W Isl 3F 63
Duncow Dum 5G 11
Duncrievie Per 3C 26
Dundee D'dee 72 (5B 34)
Dundee Airport D'dee 1E 27
Dundonald S Ayr 5G 17
Dundonnell High 5F 53
Dundraw Cumb 4F 7
Dundreggan High 2E 39
Dundrennan Dum 4A 6
Dunecht Abers 3C 42
Dunfermline Fife 73 (5B 26)
Dunino Fife 2G 27
Dunipace Falk 5H 25
Dunira Per 1G 25
Dunkeld Per 4F 33
Dunlappie Ang 2C 34
Dunlichity Lodge
High 5H 47
Dunlop E Ayr 4H 17
Dunmaglass Lodge
High 1G 39
Dunmore Arg 2A 16
Dunmore Falk 5H 25
Dunmore High 4G 47
Dunnet High 1F 59
Dunnichen Ang 4C 34
Dunning Per 2B 26
Dunoon Arg 1E 17
Dunphail Mor 4D 48
Dunragit Dum 3C 4
Dunrostan Arg 5E 23
Duns Bord 3E 21
Dunscore Dum 5F 11
Dunshalt Fife 2D 26
Dunshillock Abers 4E 51
Dunsyre S Lan 4F 19
Duntocher W Dun 1H 17
Duntulm High 1D 44
Dunure S Ayr 2H 9
Dunvegan High 4B 44
Durdar Cumb 3H 7
Durisdeer Dum 3F 11
Durisdeermill Dum 3F 11
Durnamuck High 4F 53
Durness High 2F 57
Durno Abers 1C 42
Duror High 3C 30
Durran Arg 3G 23
Durran High 2E 59
Dury Shet 1D 66
Duthil High 1C 40
Dyce Aber 2D 42
Dyke Mor 3C 48
Dykehead Ang 2A 34
Dykehead N Lan 2D 18
Dykehead Stir 4E 25
Dykend Ang 3H 33
Dykesfield Cumb 3G 7
Dysart Fife 4E 27

E

Eadar Dha Fhadhail W Isl 1B 62
Eaglesfield Cumb 5D 6
Eaglesfield Dum 1F 7
Eaglesham E Ren 3A 18
Eallabus Arg 2E 15
Earlais High 2C 44
Earle Nmbd 5G 21
Earlish High 2C 44
Earlsferry Fife 3F 27
Earlsford Abers 5D 50
Earlston E Ayr 5H 17
Earlston Bord 5C 20
Earlstoun Dum 5D 10
Earlyvale Bord 3H 19
Earsairidh W Isl 5C 60
Easdale Arg 2E 23
Eassie Ang 4A 34
Eassie and Nevay Ang 4A 34
East Barns E Lot 1E 21
East Bennan N Ayr 1E 9
East Burrafirth Shet 1C 66
East Calder W Lot 2F 19
East Clyne High 3F 55
East Clyth High 5F 59
East Croachy High 1H 39
Easter Ardross High 1H 47
Easter Balgedie Per 3C 26
Easter Balmoral Abers 4F 41
Easter Brae High 2H 47
Easter Buckieburn Stir 5G 25
Easter Fearn High 5D 54
Easter Galcantray High 4B 48
Easterhouse Glas 2B 18
Easter Howgate Midl 2H 19
Easter Kinkell High 3G 47
Easter Lednathie Ang 2A 34
Easter Ogil Ang 2B 34
Easter Ord Abers 3D 42
Easter Quarff Shet 3D 66
Easter Rhynd Per 2C 26
Easter Skeld Shet 2C 66
Easter Suddie High 3H 47
Easter Tulloch Abers 1E 35
Eastfield N Lan
nr. Caldercruix 2D 18
Eastfield N Lan
nr. Harthill 2D 18
Eastfield S Lan 2B 18
East Fortune E Lot 1C 20
East Haven Ang 5C 34
East Helmsdale High 2H 55
East Horton Nmbd 5H 21
Easthouses Midl 2A 20
East Kilbride S Lan 3B 18
East Kyloe Nmbd 5H 21
East Langwell High 3E 55
East Learmouth Nmbd 5F 21
East Linton E Lot 1C 20
East Mains Abers 4B 42
East Mey High 1G 59
Easton Cumb
nr. Burgh by Sands 3F 7
Easton Cumb
nr. Longtown 1H 7
East Ord Nmbd 3G 21
East Pitcorthie Fife 3G 27
East Rhidorroch Lodge
High 4H 53
Eastriggs Dum 2F 7
East Saltoun E Lot 2B 20
Eastshore Shet 5C 66
East Wemyss Fife 4E 27
East Whitburn W Lot 2E 19
Eastwick Shet 5G 67
East Woodburn Nmbd 5H 13
Ecclefechan Dum 1E 7
Eccles Bord 4E 21
Ecclesmachan W Lot 1F 19
Echt Abers 3C 42
Eckford Bord 1G 13
Eday Airport Orkn 1E 64
Edderside Cumb 4E 7
Edderton High 5E 55
Eddleston Bord 4H 19
Eddlewood S Lan 3C 18
Edendonich Arg 1A 24
Edentaggart Arg 4C 24
Edgehead Midl 2A 20
Edinbane High 3C 44
Edinburgh Edin 74 (1H 19)
Edinburgh Airport Edin 1G 19
Edmonstone Orkn 2E 64
Ednam Bord 5E 21
Edrom Bord 3F 21
Edzell Ang 2D 34
Effirth Shet 1C 66
Efstigarth Shet 3H 67
Eight Mile Burn Midl 3G 19
Eignaig High 4A 30
Eilanreach High 2H 37
Eildon Bord 5C 20
Eileanach Lodge High 2G 47
Eilean Fhlodaigh W Isl 5J 61
Eilean Iarmain High 2G 37
Einacleit W Isl 2C 62
Eisgein W Isl 3E 62
Elcho Per 1C 26
Elderslie Ren 2H 17
Elgin Mor 2F 49
Elgol High 2E 37
Elie Fife 3F 27
Elishaw Nmbd 4H 13
Elizafield Dum 1D 6
Ellan High 1B 40
Ellary Arg 1A 16
Ellemford Bord 2E 21
Ellenabeich Arg 2E 23
Ellenborough Cumb 5D 6
Elleric Arg 4D 30
Elliot Ang 5D 34
Ellishadder High 2E 45
Ellon Abers 5E 51
Ellonby Cumb 5H 7
Elphin High 2H 53
Elphinstone E Lot 1A 20
Elrick Abers 3D 42
Elrick Mor 1H 41
Elrig Dum 4E 5
Elsrickle S Lan 4F 19
Elvanfoot S Lan 2G 11
Elvingston E Lot 1B 20
Elwick Nmbd 5H 21
Embleton Cumb 5E 7
Embo High 4F 55
Embo Street High 4F 55
Enoch Dum 3F 11
Enochdhu Per 2F 33
Ensay Arg 4E 29
Enterkinfoot Dum 3F 11
Eolaigearraidh W Isl 4C 60
Eorabus Arg 1A 22
Europaidh W Isl 1K 63
Erbusaig High 1G 37
Erchless Castle High 4F 47
Eredine Arg 3G 23
Eriboll High 3F 57
Ericstane Dum 2H 11
Erines Arg 1B 16
Errogie High 1G 39
Errol Per 1D 26
Errol Station Per 1D 26
Erskine Ren 1H 17
Erskine Bridge Ren 1H 17
Ervie Dum 2B 4
Eskadale High 5F 47
Eskbank Midl 2A 20
Eskdalemuir Dum 4B 12
Esknish Arg 2E 15
Essich High 5H 47
Eswick Shet 1D 66
Etal Nmbd 5G 21
Ethie Haven Ang 4D 34
Etteridge High 4H 39
Ettrick Bord 2B 12
Ettrickbridge Bord 1C 12
Evanton High 2H 47
Evelix High 4E 55
Everbay Orkn 5J 65
Evertown Dum 1G 7
Ewes Dum 4C 12
Exnaboe Shet 5C 66
Eyemouth Bord 2G 21
Eynort High 1C 36
Eyre High
on Isle of Skye 3D 44
Eyre High
on Raasay 5E 45

F

Faichem High 3D 38
Faifley W Dun 1A 18
Fail S Ayr 1B 10
Failford S Ayr 1B 10
Fair Hill Cumb 5H 7
Fairhill S Lan 3C 18
Fair Isle Airport Shet 1J 65
Fairlie N Ayr 3F 17
Fairmilehead Edin 2H 19
Fala Midl 2B 20
Fala Dam Midl 2B 20
Falkirk Falk 81 (5H 25)
Falkland Fife 3D 26
Fallin Stir 4H 25
Falstone Nmbd 5G 13
Fanagmore High 4C 56
Fanellan High 4F 47
Fankerton Falk 5G 25
Fanmore Arg 4F 29
Fannich Lodge High 2D 46
Fans Bord 4D 20
Farley High 4F 47
Farmtown Mor 3A 50
Farnell Ang 3D 34
Farr High
nr. Bettyhill 2A 58
Farr High
nr. Inverness 5H 47
Farr High
nr. Kingussie 3B 40
Farraline High 1G 39
Fasag High 3H 45
Fascadale High 1G 29
Fasnacloich Arg 4D 30
Fassfern High 1D 30
Fauldhouse W Lot 2E 19
Feagour High 4G 39
Fearann Dhomhnaill High 3F 37
Fearn High 1B 48
Fearnan Per 4C 32
Fearnbeg High 3G 45
Fearnmore High 2G 45
Felkington Nmbd 4G 21
Fell Side Cumb 5G 7
Fenham Nmbd 4H 21
Fenton Cumb 3H 7
Fenton Nmbd 5G 21
Fenton Barns E Lot 5G 27
Fenwick E Ayr 4H 17
Fenwick Nmbd 4H 21
Feochaig Arg 2C 8
Feolin Ferry Arg 2F 15
Feorlan Arg 3B 8
Ferindonald High 3F 37
Feriniquarrie High 3A 44
Fern Ang 2B 34
Ferness High 4C 48
Fernieflatt Abers 1F 35
Ferniegair S Lan 3C 18
Fernilea High 5C 44
Ferryden Ang 3E 35
Ferryhill Aber 3E 43
Ferryton High 2H 47
Fersit High 1G 31
Feshiebridge High 3B 40
Fetterangus Abers 3E 51
Fettercairn Abers 1D 34
Fiag Lodge High 1B 54
Fidden Arg 1A 22
Fieldhead Cumb 5H 7
Fife Keith Mor 3H 49
Finavon Ang 3B 34
Fincharn Arg 3G 23
Findhorn Mor 2D 48
Findhorn Bridge High 1B 40
Findochty Mor 2H 49
Findo Gask Per 1B 26
Findon Abers 4E 43
Findon Mains High 2H 47
Fingland Cumb 3F 7
Fingland Dum 2E 11
Finiskaig High 4H 37
Finnart Per 3A 32
Finnygaud Abers 3B 50
Finstown Orkn 3C 64
Fintry Abers 3C 50
Fintry D'dee 5B 34
Fintry Stir 5F 25
Finzean Abers 4B 42
Fionnphort Arg 1A 22
Fionnsabhagh W Isl 6B 62
First Coast High 4E 53
Firth Shet 5H 67
Fishcross Clac 4A 26
Fisherford Abers 5B 50
Fisherrow E Lot 1A 20
Fisherton High 3A 48
Fisherton S Ayr 2H 9
Fishnish Arg 4H 29
Fishwick Bord 3G 21
Fiskavaig High 5C 44
Fitch Shet 2C 66
Fiunary High 4H 29
Fladda Shet 4G 67
Fladdabister Shet 3D 66
Flashader High 3C 44
The Flatt Cumb 5E 13
Fleck Shet 5C 66
Fleisirin W Isl 4K 63
Flemington S Lan
nr. Glasgow 2B 18
Flemington S Lan
nr. Strathaven 4C 18
Fleoideabhagh W Isl 6B 62
Fletchertown Cumb 4F 7
Fleuchary High 4E 55
Flimby Cumb 5D 6
Flodden Nmbd 5G 21
Flodigarry High 1D 44
Flushing Abers 4F 51
Fochabers Mor 3G 49
Fodderty High 3G 47
Foffarty Ang 4B 34
Fogo Bord 4E 21
Fogorig Bord 4E 21
Foindle High 4C 56
Folda Ang 2G 33
Folla Rule Abers 5C 50
Foodieash Fife 2E 27
Footdee Aber 3E 43
Forbestown Abers 2G 41
Ford Arg 3F 23
Ford Nmbd 5G 21
Fordell Fife 5C 26
Fordie Per 1G 25
Fordoun Abers 1E 35
Fordyce Abers 2A 50
Foresterseat Mor 3E 49
Forest Lodge Per 1E 33
Forest Mill Clac 4A 26
Forfar Ang 3B 34
Forgandenny Per 2B 26
Forgewood N Lan 3C 18
Forgie Mor 3G 49
Forgue Abers 4B 50
Forneth Per 4F 33
Forres Mor 3D 48
Forrestfield N Lan 2D 18
Forrest Lodge Dum 5C 10
Forse High 5F 59
Forsinard High 4B 58
Forss High 2D 58
Fort Augustus High 3E 39
Forteviot Per 2B 26
Fort George High 3A 48
Forth S Lan 3E 19
Forth Road Bridge Edin 1G 19
Fortingall Per 4C 32
Fort Matilda Inv 1F 17
Fortrie Abers 4B 50
Fortrose High 3A 48
Fort William High 81 (1E 31)
Foss Per 3C 32
Fothergill Cumb 5D 6
Foubister Orkn 4E 64
Foula Airport Shet 5A 66
Foulbridge Cumb 4H 7
Foulden Bord 3G 21
Fountainbridge Edin 7B 74
Fountainhall Bord 4B 20
Foveran Abers 1E 43
Fowlershill Aber 2E 43
Fowlis Ang 5A 34
Fowlis Wester Per 1A 26
Foyers High 1F 39
Foynesfield High 3B 48
Fraserburgh Abers 2E 51
Freester Shet 1D 66
Frenich Stir 3D 24
Fresgoe High 2C 58
Freswick High 2G 59
Freuchie Fife 3D 26
Friockheim Ang 4C 34
Frobost W Isl 2C 60
Frotoft Orkn 2D 64
Fullwood E Ayr 3H 17
Funzie Shet 3K 67
Furnace Arg 3H 23
Fyvie Abers 5C 50

G

Gabhsann bho Dheas W Isl 2J 63
Gabhsann bho Thuath
W Isl 2J 63
Gabroc Hill E Ayr 3H 17
Gadgirth S Ayr 1B 10
Gaick Lodge High 5A 40
Gairletter Arg 5A 24
Gairloch Abers 3C 42
Gairloch High 1H 45
Gairlochy High 5C 38
Gairney Bank Per 4C 26
Gairnshiel Lodge Abers 3F 41
Gaitsgill Cumb 4G 7
Galashiels Bord 5B 20
Gallatown Fife 4D 26
Gallin Per 4A 32
Gallowfauld Ang 4B 34
Gallowhill Per 5G 33
Gallowhill Ren 2H 17
Gallowhills Abers 3F 51
Galltair High 1H 37
Galmisdale High 5D 36
Galston E Ayr 5H 17
Galtrigill High 3A 44
Gamelsby Cumb 3F 7
Ganavan Arg 5B 30
Gannochy Ang 1C 34
Gannochy Per 1C 26
Gansclet High 4G 59
Garafad High 2D 44
Gardenstown Abers 2D 50
Garderhouse Shet 2C 66
Gardie Shet
on Papa Stour 1A 66
Gardie Shet
on Unst 1K 67
Gardie Ho Shet 2D 66
Garelochhead Arg 4B 24
Gargunnock Stir 4G 25
Garleffin S Ayr 5F 9
Garlieston Dum 4F 5
Garlogie Abers 3C 42
Garmond Abers 3D 50
Garmony Arg 4H 29
Garmouth Mor 2G 49
Garnethill Glas 3D 78
Garnkirk N Lan 2B 18
Garrabost W Isl 4K 63
Garrallan E Ayr 2C 10
Garrogie Lodge High 2G 39
Garros High 2D 44
Garrow Per 4D 32
Gartcosh N Lan 2B 18
Garth Shet
nr. Sandness 1B 66
Garth Shet
nr. Skellister 1D 66
Garthamlock Glas 2B 18
Gartly Abers 5A 50
Gartmore Stir 4E 25
Gartness N Lan 2C 18
Gartness Stir 5E 25
Gartocharn W Dun 5D 24
Gartsherrie N Lan 2C 18
Gartymore High 2H 55
Garvald E Lot 1C 20
Garvamore High 4G 39
Garvard Arg 4A 22
Garvault High 5A 58
Garve High 2E 47
Garvie Arg 4H 23
Garvock Abers 1E 35
Garvock Inv 1F 17
Gaskan High 1B 30
Gatehead E Ayr 5G 17
Gatehouse Nmbd 5G 13
Gatehouse of Fleet Dum 3H 5
Gatelawbridge Dum 4G 11
Gateside Ang
nr. Forfar 4B 34
Gateside Ang
nr. Kirriemuir 4A 34
Gateside Fife 3C 26
Gateside N Ayr 3G 17
Gattonside Bord 5C 20
Gauldry Fife 1E 27
Gavinton Bord 3E 21
Gayfield Edin 1H 74
Gayfield Orkn 2G 65
Geanies High 1B 48
Gearraidh Bhailteas W Isl 2C 60
Gearraidh Bhaird W Isl 3E 62
Gearraidh ma Monadh
W Isl 3C 60
Gearraidh na h-Aibhne
W Isl 1D 62
Geary High 2B 44
Geddes High 3B 48
Gedintailor High 5E 45
Geilston Arg 1G 17
Geirinis W Isl 6H 61
Geise High 2E 59
Geisiadar W Isl 1C 62
Gelder Shiel Abers 5F 41
Gellyburn Per 5F 33
Gelston Dum 3A 6
Geocrab W Isl 5C 62
Georgetown Ren 2H 17
Georth Orkn 2C 64
Gerston High 3E 59
Giffnock E Ren 3A 18
Gifford E Lot 2C 20
Giffordtown Fife 2D 26
Gilchriston E Lot 2B 20
Gilcrux Cumb 5E 7
Gillen High 3B 44
Gillock High 3F 59
Gills High 1G 59
Gilmanscleuch Bord 1C 12
Gilmerton Edin 2H 19
Gilmerton Per 1H 25
Gilston Bord 3B 20
Giosla W Isl 2C 62
Girdle Toll N Ayr 4G 17
Girlsta Shet 1D 66
Girthon Dum 3H 5
Girvan S Ayr 4G 9
Gladsmuir E Lot 1B 20
Glaichbea High 5G 47
Glame High 4E 45
Glamis Ang 4A 34
Glas Aird Arg 4A 22
Glas-allt Shiel Abers 5F 41
Glaschoil High 5D 48
Glasgow Glas 78 (2A 18)
Glasgow Airport Ren 2H 17
Glasgow Prestwick Airport
S Ayr 1A 10
Glashvin High 2D 44
Glas na Cardaich High 4F 37
Glasnacardoch High 4F 37
Glasnakille High 2E 37
Glassburn High 5E 47
Glasserton Dum 5F 5
Glassford S Lan 4C 18
Glassgreen Mor 2F 49
Glasson Cumb 2F 7
Glasterlaw Ang 3C 34
Gleann Dail bho Dheas
W Isl 3C 60
Gleann Tholastaidh W Isl 3K 63
Gleann Uige High 1H 29
Glecknabae Arg 2D 16
Glen Dum 3G 5
Glenancross High 4F 37
Glenbarr Arg 5H 15
Glenbeg High 2G 29
Glen Bernisdale High 4D 44
Glenbervie Abers 5C 42
Glenboig N Lan 2C 18
Glenborrodale High 2H 29
Glenbranter Arg 4A 24
Glenbreck Bord 1H 11
Glenbrein Lodge High 2F 39
Glenbrittle High 1D 36
Glenbuchat Lodge Abers 2G 41
Glenbuck E Ayr 1E 11
Glenburn Ren 2H 17
Glencalvie Lodge High 5B 54
Glencaple Dum 2C 6
Glencarron Lodge High 3B 46
Glencarse Per 1C 26
Glencassley Castle High 3B 54
Glencat Abers 4A 42
Glencoe High 3E 31
Glen Cottage High 5F 37
Glencraig Fife 4C 26
Glendale High 4A 44
Glendevon Per 3A 26
Glendoebeg High 3F 39
Glendoick Per 1D 26
Glendoune S Ayr 4G 9
Glenduckie Fife 2D 26
Gleneagles Per 3A 26
Glenegedale Arg 3E 15
Glenegedale Lots Arg 3E 15
Glenelg High 2H 37
Glenernie Mor 4D 48
Glenesslin Dum 5F 11
Glenfarg Per 2C 26
Glenfarquhar Lodge Abers 5C 42
Glenferness Mains High 4C 48
Glenfeshie Lodge High 4B 40
Glenfiddich Lodge Mor 5G 49
Glenfinnan High 5A 38
Glenfintaig Lodge High 5D 38
Glenfoot Per 2C 26
Glenfyne Lodge Arg 2B 24
Glengap Dum 3H 5
Glengarnock N Ayr 3G 17
Glengolly High 2E 59
Glengorm Castle Arg 3F 29
Glengrasco High 4D 44
Glenhead Farm Ang 2H 33
Glenholm Bord 5G 19
Glen House Bord 5H 19
Glenhurich High 2B 30
Glenkerry Bord 2B 12
Glenkiln Dum 1B 6
Glenkindie Abers 2H 41
Glenkinglass Lodge Arg 5E 31
Glenkirk Bord 1H 11
Glenlean Arg 5H 23
Glenlee Dum 5D 10
Glenleraig High 5C 56
Glenlichorn Per 2G 25
Glenlivet Mor 1E 41
Glenlochar Dum 2A 6
Glenlochsie Lodge Per 1F 33
Glenluce Dum 3C 4
Glenmarksie High 3E 47
Glenmassan Arg 5A 24
Glenmavis N Lan 2C 18
Glenmazeran Lodge High 1A 40
Glenmidge Dum 5F 11
Glenmore High
nr. Glenborrodale 2G 29
Glenmore High
nr. Kingussie 3C 40
Glenmore High
on Isle of Skye 4D 44
Glenmoy Ang 2B 34
Glennoe Arg 5D 30
Glen of Coachford Abers 4H 49
Glenogil Ang 2B 34
Glenprosen Village Ang 2A 34
Glenree N Ayr 1E 9
Glenrosa N Ayr 5D 16
Glenrothes Fife 3D 26
Glensanda High 4B 30
Glensaugh Abers 1D 34
Glenshero Lodge High 4G 39
Glensluain Arg 4H 23
Glenstockadale Dum 2B 4
Glenstriven Arg 1D 16
Glen Tanar House Abers 4H 41
Glenton Abers 1B 42
Glentress Bord 5H 19
Glentromie Lodge High 4A 40
Glentrool Lodge Dum 5B 10
Glentrool Village Dum 1E 5
Glentruim House High 4H 39
Glenuig High 1H 29
Glen Village Falk 1D 18
Glenwhilly Dum 1C 4
Glenzierfoot Dum 1G 7
Glespin S Lan 1F 11
Gletness Shet 1D 66
Glib Cheois W Isl 2E 62
Gloup Shet 2J 67
Glutt Lodge High 5C 58
Gobernuisgach Lodge High 4F 57
Gobernuisgeach High 5C 58
Gobhaig W Isl 4B 62
Gogar Edin 1G 19
Gollanfield High 3B 48
Golspie High 4F 55
Gometra House Arg 4E 29
Gonfirth Shet 6G 67
Gord Shet 4D 66

Gordon—Kinloid

Gordon *Bord* 4D **20**
Gordonbush *High* 3F **55**
Gordonstown *Abers*
nr. Cornhill 3A **50**
Gordonstown *Abers*
nr. Fyvie 5C **50**
Gorebridge *Midl* 2A **20**
Gorgie *Edin* 1H **19**
Gorseness *Orkn* 3D **64**
Gorstan *High* 2E **47**
Gortantaoid *Arg* 1E **15**
Gorteneorn *High* 2H **29**
Gortenfern *High* 2H **29**
Gossabrough *Shet* 4J **67**
Goswick *Nmbd* 4H **21**
Gott *Arg* 4B **28**
Gott *Shet* 2D **66**
Gourdon *Abers* 1F **35**
Gourock *Inv* 1F **17**
Govan *Glas* 2A **18**
Govanhill *Glas* 2A **18**
Gowanhill *Abers* 2F **51**
Gowkhall *Fife* 5B **26**
Grabhair *W Isl* 3E **62**
Gramasdail *W Isl* 5J **61**
Grandtully *Per* 3E **33**
Grange *E Ayr* 5H **17**
Grange *Per* 1D **26**
Grange Crossroads *Mor* 3H **49**
Grangemouth *Falk* 5A **26**
Grange of Lindores *Fife* 2D **26**
Grangepans *Falk* 5B **26**
Granish *High* 2B **40**
Grantlodge *Abers* 2C **42**
Granton *Edin* 1H **19**
Grantown-on-Spey *High* 1D **40**
Grantshouse *Bord* 2F **21**
Grassgarth *Cumb* 4G **7**
Graven *Shet* 5H **67**
Grealin *High* 2E **45**
Great Blencow *Cumb* 5H **7**
Great Broughton *Cumb* 5D **6**
Great Clifton *Cumb* 5D **6**
Great Corby *Cumb* 3H **7**
Great Orton *Cumb* 3G **7**
Greenbank *Shet* 2J **67**
Greenburn *W Lot* 2E **19**
Greendykes *Nmbd* 5H **21**
Greenfield *Arg* 4B **24**
Greenfoot *N Lan* 2C **18**
Greengairs *N Lan* 1C **18**
Greengill *Cumb* 5E **7**
Greenhaugh *Nmbd* 5G **13**
Greenhill *Dum* 1E **7**
Greenhill *Falk* 1D **18**
Greenhills *N Ayr* 3G **17**
Greenholm *E Ayr* 5A **18**
Greenigoe *Orkn* 4D **64**
Greenland *High* 2F **59**
Greenland Mains *High* 2F **59**
Greenlaw *Bord* 4E **21**
Greenlea *Dum* 1D **6**
Greenloaning *Per* 3H **25**
Greenmow *Shet* 4D **66**
Greenock *Inv* 1F **17**
Greenock Mains *E Ayr* 1D **10**
Greenrow *Cumb* 3E **7**
Greens *Abers* 4D **50**
Greenside *Edin* 2H **74**
Greenwall *Orkn* 4E **64**
Grein *W Isl* 4B **60**
Greinetobht *W Isl* 3J **61**
Gremista *Shet* 2D **66**
Greosabhagh *W Isl* 5C **62**
Greshornish *High* 3C **44**
Gretna *Dum* 2G **7**
Gretna Green *Dum* 2G **7**
Greysouthen *Cumb* 5D **6**
Greystoke *Cumb* 5H **7**
Greystoke Gill *Cumb* 5H **7**
Greystone *Ang* 4C **34**
Griais *W Isl* 3J **63**
Grianan *W Isl* 4J **63**
Gribun *Arg* 5F **29**
Grimbister *Orkn* 3C **64**
Grimeston *Orkn* 3C **64**
Griminis *W Isl*
on Benbecula 5H **61**
Griminis *W Isl*
on North Uist 3H **61**
Grimister *Shet* 3H **67**
Grimness *Orkn* 5D **64**
Grindiscol *Shet* 3D **66**
Grindon *Nmbd* 4G **21**
Grinsdale *Cumb* 3G **7**
Griomsidar *W Isl* 5J **63**
Grishipoll *Arg* 3C **28**
Gritley *Orkn* 4E **64**
Grobister *Orkn* 5J **65**
Grobsness *Shet* 6G **67**
Grogport *Arg* 4B **16**
Groigearraidh *W Isl* 6H **61**
The Grove *Dum* 1C **6**
Grudie *High* 2E **47**
Gruids *High* 3C **54**
Gruinard House *High* 4E **53**
Gruinart *Arg* 2D **14**
Grulinbeg *Arg* 2D **14**
Gruline *Arg* 4G **29**
Grummore *High* 5H **57**
Gruting *Shet* 2B **66**
Grutness *Shet* 6D **66**
Gualachulain *High* 4E **31**
Gualin House *High* 3E **57**
Guardbridge *Fife* 2F **27**
Guay *Per* 4F **33**
Guildtown *Per* 5G **33**
Gulberwick *Shet* 3D **66**
Gullane *E Lot* 5F **27**
Gunnerton *Nmbd* 5H **13**
Gunnista *Shet* 2D **66**
Gunsgreenhill *Bord* 2G **21**
Gutcher *Shet* 3J **67**
Guthrie *Ang* 3C **34**

H

Haa of Houlland *Shet* 2J **67**
Hackland *Orkn* 2C **64**
Hackness *Orkn* 5C **64**
Haclait *W Isl* 6J **61**
Hadden *Bord* 5E **21**
Haddington *E Lot* 1C **20**
Haddo *Abers* 5D **50**
Haggbeck *Cumb* 1H **7**
Haggersta *Shet* 2C **66**
Haggerston *Nmbd* 4H **21**
Haggrister *Shet* 5G **67**
Halbeath *Fife* 5C **26**
Halcro *High* 2F **59**
Halistra *High* 3B **44**
Halket *E Ayr* 3H **17**
Halkirk *High* 3E **59**
Hall *E Ren* 3H **17**
Halliburton *Bord* 4D **20**
Hallin *High* 3B **44**
Hallyne *Bord* 4G **19**
Haltcliff Bridge *Cumb* 5G **7**
Ham *High* 1F **59**
Ham *Shet* 5A **66**
Hamilton *S Lan* **82** (3C **18**)
Hamister *Shet* 6J **67**
Hamnavoe *Shet*
nr. Braehoulland 4F **67**
Hamnavoe *Shet*
nr. Burland 3C **66**
Hamnavoe *Shet*
nr. Lunna 5H **67**
Hamnavoe *Shet*
on Yell 4H **67**
Happas *Ang* 4B **34**
Happendon *S Lan* 5D **18**
Hardgate *Abers* 3C **42**
Hardgate *Dum* 2B **6**
Harelaw *Dum* 1H **7**
Hareshaw *N Lan* 2D **18**
Harker *Cumb* 2G **7**
Harkland *Shet* 4H **67**
Harlosh *High* 4B **44**
Haroldswick *Shet* 1K **67**
Harpsdale *High* 3E **59**
Harraby *Cumb* 3H **7**
Harrapool *High* 1F **37**
Harrapul *High* 1F **37**
Harrietfield *Per* 1A **26**
Harrington *Cumb* 5C **6**
Harriston *Cumb* 4E **7**
Harthill *N Lan* 2E **19**
Hartmount Holdings
High 1A **48**
Hartwood *N Lan* 3D **18**
Hassendean *Bord* 1E **13**
Haster *High* 3G **59**
Hastigrow *High* 2F **59**
Hatton *Abers* 5F **51**
Hattoncrook *Abers* 1D **42**
Hatton of Fintray *Abers* 2D **42**
Haugh *E Ayr* 1B **10**
Haugh Head *Nmbd* 5H **21**
Haugh of Ballechin *Per* 3E **33**
Haugh of Glass *Mor* 5H **49**
Haugh of Urr *Dum* 2B **6**
Haunn *Arg* 4E **29**
Haunn *W Isl* 3C **60**
Hawick *Bord* 2E **13**
Hawksdale *Cumb* 4G **7**
Hayhill *E Ayr* 2B **10**
Hayshead *Ang* 4D **34**
Hayton *Aber* 3E **43**
Hayton *Cumb*
nr. Aspatria 4E **7**
Hayton *Cumb*
nr. Brampton 3H **7**
Haywood *S Lan* 3E **19**
Hazelbank *S Lan* 4D **18**
Hazelton Walls *Fife* 1E **27**
Head of Muir *Falk* 5H **25**
Heads Nook *Cumb* 3H **7**
Heanish *Arg* 4B **28**
Heaste *High* 2F **37**
Heatherfield *High* 4D **44**
Heathfield *Cumb* 4E **7**
Heathfield *Ren* 2G **17**
Heathhall *Dum* 1C **6**
Heck *Dum* 5H **11**
Heddle *Orkn* 3C **64**
Heglibister *Shet* 1C **66**
Heights of Brae *High* 2G **47**
Heights of Fodderty *High* 2G **47**
Heights of Kinlochewe
High 2B **46**
Heiton *Bord* 5E **21**
Helensburgh *Arg* 5B **24**
Hellister *Shet* 2C **66**
Helmsdale *High* 2H **55**
Hempriggs *High* 4G **59**
Heogan *Shet* 2D **66**
Heribusta *High* 1D **44**
Heriot *Bord* 3B **20**
Hermiston *Edin* 1G **19**
Hermitage *Bord* 4E **13**
Heronsford *S Ayr* 5G **9**
Herra *Shet* 3K **67**
Herston *Orkn* 5D **64**
Hesket Newmarket
Cumb 5G **7**
Hesleyside *Nmbd* 5H **13**
Hessilhead *N Ayr* 3G **17**
Hestaford *Shet* 1B **66**
Hestinsetter *Shet* 2B **66**
Hestwall *Orkn* 3B **64**
Hethersgill *Cumb* 2H **7**
Hetherside *Cumb* 2H **7**
Hethpool *Nmbd* 1H **13**
Hetton Steads *Nmbd* 5H **21**
Heugh-head *Abers* 2G **41**
Heylipol *Arg* 4A **28**
High Auldgirth *Dum* 5G **11**
High Banton *N Lan* 5G **25**
High Blantyre *S Lan* 3B **18**
High Bonnybridge *Falk* 1D **18**
Highbridge *Cumb* 4G **7**
Highbridge *High* 5D **38**
High Crosby *Cumb* 3H **7**
Highfield *N Ayr* 3G **17**
High Gallowhill *E Dun* 1B **18**
Highgate *N Ayr* 3G **17**
Highgreen Manor
Nmbd 4H **13**
High Harrington *Cumb* 5D **6**
High Hesket *Cumb* 4H **7**
High Ireby *Cumb* 5F **7**
High Keil *Arg* 3B **8**
Highlaws *Cumb* 4E **7**
High Longthwaite *Cumb* 4F **7**
High Lorton *Cumb* 5E **7**
Highmoor *Cumb* 4F **7**
High Row *Cumb* 5G **7**
High Scales *Cumb* 4E **7**
High Side *Cumb* 5F **7**
Hightae *Dum* 1D **6**
High Valleyfield *Fife* 5B **26**
Hillbrae *Abers*
nr. Aberchirder 4B **50**
Hillbrae *Abers*
nr. Inverurie 1C **42**
Hillbrae *Abers*
nr. Methlick 5D **50**
Hill End *Fife* 4B **26**
Hillend *Fife* 5C **26**
Hillend *N Lan* 2D **18**
Hillhead *Abers* 5A **50**
Hillhead *S Ayr* 2B **10**
Hillhead of Auchentumb
Abers 3E **51**
Hilliclay *High* 2E **59**
Hillington *Glas* 2A **18**
Hill of Beath *Fife* 4C **26**
Hill of Fearn *High* 1B **48**
Hill of Fiddes *Abers* 1E **43**
Hill of Keillor *Ang* 4H **33**
Hill of Overbrae *Abers* 2D **50**
Hillside *Abers* 4E **43**
Hillside *Ang* 2E **35**
Hillside *Orkn* 2C **64**
Hillside *Shet* 6H **67**
Hillside of Prieston *Ang* 5A **34**
Hillswick *Shet* 5F **67**
Hillwell *Shet* 5C **66**
Hillyland *Per* 1B **26**
Hilton *High* 5E **55**
Hilton of Cadboll *High* 1B **48**
Hirn *Abers* 3C **42**
Hirst *N Lan* 2D **18**
Hobbister *Orkn* 4C **64**
Hobkirk *Bord* 2E **13**
Hoddomcross *Dum* 1E **7**
Hogaland *Shet* 5G **67**
Hogha Gearraidh *W Isl* 3H **61**
Holburn *Nmbd* 5H **21**
Holland *Orkn*
on Papa Westray 2G **65**
Holland *Orkn*
on Stronsay 5J **65**
Hollandstoun *Orkn* 2K **65**
Hollows *Dum* 1G **7**
Hollybush *E Ayr* 2A **10**
Holmend *Dum* 3H **11**
Holme St Cuthbert *Cumb* 4E **7**
Holmhead *E Ayr* 1C **10**
Holmisdale *High* 4A **44**
Holm of Drumlanrig
Dum 4F **11**
Holmsgarth *Shet* 2D **66**
Holmwrangle *Cumb* 4H **7**
Holytown *N Lan* 2C **18**
Holywood *Dum* 5G **11**
Hoove *Shet* 2C **66**
Hope *High* 2F **57**
Hopeman *Mor* 2E **49**
Horgabost *W Isl* 5B **62**
Horncliffe *Nmbd* 4G **21**
Horndean *Bord* 4F **21**
Hornsby *Cumb* 3H **7**
Hornsbygate *Cumb* 3H **7**
Horsbrugh Ford *Bord* 5H **19**
Horsley *Nmbd* 4H **13**
Horsleyhill *Bord* 2E **13**
Hosh *Per* 1H **25**
Hosta *W Isl* 3H **61**
Hoswick *Shet* 4D **66**
Houbie *Shet* 3K **67**
Hough *Arg* 4A **28**
Houghton *Cumb* 3H **7**
Houlland *Shet*
on Mainland 1C **66**
Houlland *Shet*
on Yell 5J **67**
Houndslow *Bord* 4D **20**
Houndwood *Bord* 2F **21**
Housabister *Shet* 1D **66**
Housay *Shet* 5K **67**
Househill *High* 3B **48**
Housetter *Shet* 4G **67**
Houss *Shet* 3C **66**
Houston *Ren* 2H **17**
Housty *High* 5E **59**
Houton *Orkn* 4C **64**
How *Cumb* 3H **7**
Howe *High* 2G **59**
Howe of Teuchar
Abers 4C **50**
Howes *Dum* 2E **7**
Howgate *Midl* 3H **19**
Hownam *Bord* 2G **13**
Howtel *Nmbd* 5F **21**
Howwood *Ren* 2G **17**
Hughton *High* 4F **47**
Huisinis *W Isl* 3A **62**
Humbie *E Lot* 2B **20**
Humbleton *Nmbd* 5G **21**
Hume *Bord* 4E **21**
Huna *High* 1G **59**
Hungladder *High* 1C **44**
Hunspow *High* 1F **59**
Hunterfield *Midl* 2A **20**
Hunter's Quay *Arg* 1E **17**
Hunthill Lodge *Ang* 1B **34**
Huntington *E Lot* 1B **20**
Huntingtower *Per* 1B **26**
Huntly *Abers* 5A **50**
Huntlywood *Bord* 4D **20**
Hurlet *Glas* 2A **18**
Hurlford *E Ayr* 5H **17**
Hurliness *Orkn* 6B **64**
Hutton *Cumb* 5H **7**
Hutton *Bord* 3G **21**
Hutton End *Cumb* 5H **7**
Hutton Roof *Cumb* 5G **7**
Huxter *Shet*
on Mainland 1A **66**
Huxter *Shet*
on Whalsay 6J **67**
Hyndford Bridge *S Lan* 4E **19**
Hynish *Arg* 5A **28**
Hythie *Abers* 3F **51**

I

Ianstown *Mor* 2H **49**
Iarsiadar *W Isl* 1C **62**
Ibrox *Glas* 2A **18**
Ichrachan *Arg* 5D **30**
Idrigill *High* 2C **44**
Imachar *N Ayr* 4B **16**
Inchbae Lodge *High* 2F **47**
Inchbare *Ang* 2D **34**
Inchberry *Mor* 3G **49**
Inchbraoch *Ang* 3E **35**
Incheril *High* 2B **46**
Inchinnan *Ren* 2H **17**
Inchlaggan *High* 3C **38**
Inchmichael *Per* 1D **26**
Inchnadamph *High* 1H **53**
Inchree *High* 2D **30**
Inchture *Per* 1D **26**
Inchyra *Per* 1C **26**
Inkstack *High* 1F **59**
Innellan *Arg* 2E **17**
Innerleith *Fife* 2D **26**
Innerleithen *Bord* 5A **20**
Innerleven *Fife* 3E **27**
Innermessan *Dum* 2B **4**
Innerwick *E Lot* 1E **21**
Innerwick *Per* 4A **32**
Insch *Abers* 1B **42**
Insh *High* 3B **40**
Inshegra *High* 3D **56**
Inshore *High* 1E **57**
Inver *Abers* 4F **41**
Inver *High* 5F **55**
Inver *Per* 4F **33**
Inverailort *High* 5G **37**
Inveralligin *High* 3H **45**
Inverallochy *Abers* 2F **51**
Inveramsay *Abers* 1C **42**
Inveran *High* 4C **54**
Inveraray *Arg* 3H **23**
Inverarish *High* 5E **45**
Inverarity *Ang* 4B **34**
Inverarnan *Stir* 2C **24**
Inverarnie *High* 5H **47**
Inverbeg *Arg* 4C **24**
Inverbervie *Abers* 1F **35**
Inverboyndie *Abers* 2B **50**
Invercassley *High* 3B **54**
Invercharnan *High* 4E **31**
Inverchoran *High* 3D **46**
Invercreran *Arg* 4D **30**
Inverdruie *High* 2C **40**
Inverebrie *Abers* 5E **51**
Invereck *Arg* 5A **24**
Inveresk *E Lot* 1A **20**
Inveresragan *Arg* 5C **30**
Inverey *Abers* 5D **40**
Inverfarigaig *High* 1G **39**
Invergarry *High* 3E **39**
Invergeldie *Per* 1G **25**
Invergordon *High* 2A **48**
Invergowrie *Per* 5A **34**
Inverguseran *High* 3G **37**
Inverharroch *Mor* 5G **49**
Inverie *High* 3G **37**
Inverinan *Arg* 2G **23**
Inverinate *High* 1A **38**
Inverkeilor *Ang* 4D **34**
Inverkeithing *Fife* 5C **26**
Inverkeithny *Abers* 4B **50**
Inverkip *Inv* 1F **17**
Inverkirkaig *High* 2F **53**
Inverlael *High* 5G **53**
Inverliever Lodge *Arg* 3F **23**
Inverliver *Arg* 5D **30**
Inverlochlarig *Stir* 2D **24**
Inverlochy *High* 1E **31**
Inverlussa *Arg* 5D **22**
Inver Mallie *High* 5C **38**
Invermarkie *Abers* 5H **49**
Invermoriston *High* 2F **39**
Invernaver *High* 2A **58**
Inverneil House *Arg* 5F **23**
Inverness *High* **82** (4H **47**)
Inverness Airport
High 3A **48**
Invernettie *Abers* 4G **51**
Inverpolly Lodge
High 2F **53**
Inverquhomery
Abers 4F **51**
Inverroy *High* 5D **38**
Inversanda *High* 3C **30**
Invershiel *High* 2A **38**
Invershin *High* 4C **54**
Invershore *High* 5F **59**
Inversnaid *Stir* 3C **24**
Inverugie *Abers* 4G **51**
Inveruglas *Arg* 3C **24**
Inverurie *Abers* 1C **42**
Invervar *Per* 4B **32**
Inverythan *Abers* 4C **50**
Iochdar *W Isl* 6H **61**
Ireby *Cumb* 5F **7**
Ireland *Shet* 4C **66**
Irthington *Cumb* 2H **7**
Irvine *N Ayr* 5G **17**
Irvine Mains *N Ayr* 5G **17**
Isauld *High* 2C **58**
Isbister *Orkn* 3C **64**
Isbister *Shet*
on Mainland 3G **67**
Isbister *Shet*
on Whalsay 6J **67**
Islay Airport *Arg* 3E **15**
Isle of Whithorn *Dum* 5F **5**
Isleornsay *High* 2G **37**
Islesburgh *Shet* 6G **67**
Islesteps *Dum* 1C **6**
Islibhig *W Isl* 2A **62**
Itlaw *Abers* 3B **50**
Ivegill *Cumb* 4H **7**
Iverchaolain *Arg* 1D **16**

J

Jackton *S Lan* 3A **18**
Jamestown *Dum* 4C **12**
Jamestown *Fife* 5C **26**
Jamestown *High* 3F **47**
Jamestown *W Dun* 5C **24**
Janetstown *High*
nr. Thurso 2D **58**
Janetstown *High*
nr. Wick 3G **59**
Jedburgh *Bord* 1F **13**
Jemimaville *High* 2A **48**
Jenkins Park *High* 3E **39**
Johnby *Cumb* 5H **7**
John o' Groats *High* 1G **59**
Johnshaven *Abers* 2E **35**
Johnstone *Ren* 2H **17**
Johnstonebridge *Dum* 4H **11**
Joppa *Edin* 1A **20**
Joppa *S Ayr* 2B **10**
Juniper Green *Edin* 2G **19**

K

Kaimend *S Lan* 4E **19**
Kaimes *Edin* 2H **19**
Kaimrig End *Bord* 4F **19**
Kames *Arg* 1C **16**
Kames *E Ayr* 1D **10**
Kearvaig *High* 1D **56**
Kedlock Feus *Fife* 2E **27**
Keig *Abers* 2B **42**
Keilarsbrae *Clac* 4H **25**
Keillmore *Arg* 5D **22**
Keillor *Per* 4H **33**
Keillour *Per* 1A **26**
Keills *Arg* 2F **15**
Keiloch *Abers* 4E **41**
Keils *Arg* 2G **15**
Keir Mill *Dum* 4F **11**
Keiss *High* 2G **59**
Keith *Mor* 3H **49**
Keith Inch *Abers* 4G **51**
Kellan *Arg* 4G **29**
Kellas *Ang* 5B **34**
Kellas *Mor* 3E **49**
Kelloholm *Dum* 2E **11**
Kelsick *Cumb* 3E **7**
Kelso *Bord* 5E **21**
Keltneyburn *Per* 4C **32**
Kelton *Dum* 1C **6**
Kelton Hill *Dum* 3A **6**
Kelty *Fife* 4C **26**
Kelvinside *Glas* 2A **18**
Kemback *Fife* 2F **27**
Kemnay *Abers* 2C **42**
Kengharair *Arg* 4F **29**
Kenknock *Stir* 5H **31**
Kenmore *High* 3G **45**
Kenmore *Per* 4C **32**
Kennacraig *Arg* 2B **16**
Kennet *Clac* 4A **26**
Kennethmont *Abers* 1A **42**
Kennoway *Fife* 3E **27**
Kenovay *Arg* 4A **28**
Kensaleyre *High* 3D **44**
Kentallen *High* 3D **30**
Kentra *High* 2H **29**
Keoldale *High* 2E **57**
Keppoch *High* 1A **38**
Kerrow *High* 5E **47**
Kerrycroy *Arg* 2E **17**
Kerse *Ren* 3G **17**
Kershopefoot *Cumb* 5D **12**
Kettins *Per* 5H **33**
Kettlebridge *Fife* 3E **27**
Kettleholm *Dum* 1E **7**
Kettletoft *Orkn* 4J **65**
Keyhead *Abers* 3F **51**
Kiel Crofts *Arg* 5C **30**
Kielder *Nmbd* 4F **13**
Kilbagie *Fife* 4A **26**
Kilbarchan *Ren* 2H **17**
Kilbeg *High* 3F **37**
Kilberry *Arg* 2A **16**
Kilbirnie *N Ayr* 3G **17**
Kilbride *Arg* 1F **23**
Kilbride *High* 1E **37**
Kilbucho Place *Bord* 5F **19**
Kilchattan *Arg* 4A **22**
Kilchattan Bay *Arg* 3E **17**
Kilchenzie *Arg* 1B **8**
Kilcheran *Arg* 5B **30**
Kilchiaran *Arg* 2D **14**
Kilchoan *High*
nr. Inverie 4G **37**
Kilchoan *High*
nr. Tobermory 2F **29**
Kilchoman *Arg* 2D **14**
Kilchrenan *Arg* 1H **23**
Kilconquhar *Fife* 3F **27**
Kilcoy *High* 3G **47**
Kilcreggan *Arg* 5B **24**
Kildary *High* 1A **48**
Kildermorie Lodge *High* 1G **47**
Kildonan *Dum* 3B **4**
Kildonan *High*
nr. Helmsdale 1G **55**
Kildonan *High*
on Isle of Skye 3C **44**
Kildonan *N Ayr* 1F **9**
Kildonnan *High* 5D **36**
Kildrummy *Abers* 2H **41**
Kilfillan *Dum* 3D **4**
Kilfinan *Arg* 1C **16**
Kilfinnan *High* 4D **38**
Kilgour *Fife* 3D **26**
Kilgrammie *S Ayr* 3H **9**
Kilham *Nmbd* 5F **21**
Kilkenneth *Arg* 4A **28**
Killandrist *Arg* 4B **30**
Killean *Arg* 4H **15**
Killearn *Stir* 5E **25**
Killellan *Arg* 2B **8**
Killen *High* 3H **47**
Killichonan *Per* 3A **32**
Killiechronan *Arg* 4G **29**
Killiecrankie *Per* 2E **33**
Killilan *High* 5A **46**
Killimster *High* 3G **59**
Killin *Stir* 5A **32**
Killin Lodge *High* 3G **39**
Killinochonoch *Arg* 4F **23**
Killochyett *Bord* 4B **20**
Killundine *High* 4G **29**
Kilmacolm *Inv* 2G **17**
Kilmahog *Stir* 3F **25**
Kilmahumaig *Arg* 4E **23**
Kilmalieu *High* 3B **30**
Kilmaluag *High* 1D **44**
Kilmany *Fife* 1E **27**
Kilmarie *High* 2E **37**
Kilmarnock *E Ayr* **83** (5H **17**)
Kilmaron *Fife* 2E **27**
Kilmartin *Arg* 4F **23**
Kilmaurs *E Ayr* 4H **17**
Kilmelford *Arg* 2F **23**
Kilmeny *Arg* 2E **15**
Kilmichael Glassary *Arg* 4F **23**
Kilmichael of Inverlussa
Arg 5E **23**
Kilmoluaig *Arg* 4A **28**
Kilmorack *High* 4F **47**
Kilmore *Arg* 1F **23**
Kilmore *High* 3F **37**
Kilmory *Arg* 1A **16**
Kilmory *High*
nr. Kilchoan 1G **29**
Kilmory *High*
on Rùm 3C **36**
Kilmory *N Ayr* 1E **9**
Kilmory Lodge *Arg* 3E **23**
Kilmote *High* 2G **55**
Kilmuir *High*
nr. Dunvegan 4B **44**
Kilmuir *High*
nr. Invergordon 1A **48**
Kilmuir *High*
nr. Inverness 4H **47**
Kilmuir *High*
nr. Uig 1C **44**
Kilmun *Arg* 5A **24**
Kilnave *Arg* 1D **14**
Kilncadzow *S Lan* 4D **18**
Kilnhill *Cumb* 5F **7**
Kilninian *Arg* 4E **29**
Kilninver *Arg* 1F **23**
Kiloran *Arg* 4A **22**
Kilpatrick *N Ayr* 1E **9**
Kilrenny *Fife* 3G **27**
Kilspindie *Per* 1D **26**
Kilsyth *N Lan* 1C **18**
Kiltarlity *High* 4G **47**
Kilvaxter *High* 2C **44**
Kilwinning *N Ayr* 4F **17**
Kimmerston *Nmbd* 5G **21**
Kinbeachie *High* 2H **47**
Kinbrace *High* 5B **58**
Kinbuck *Stir* 3G **25**
Kincaple *Fife* 2F **27**
Kincardine *Fife* 5A **26**
Kincardine *High* 5D **54**
Kincardine Bridge *Falk* 5A **26**
Kincardine O'Neil *Abers* 4A **42**
Kinchrackine *Arg* 1A **24**
Kincorth *Aber* 3E **43**
Kincraig *High* 3B **40**
Kincraigie *Per* 4E **33**
Kindallachan *Per* 3E **33**
Kinfauns *Per* 1C **26**
Kingairloch *High* 3B **30**
Kingarth *Arg* 3D **16**
King Edward *Abers* 3C **50**
Kingholm Quay *Dum* 1C **6**
Kinghorn *Fife* 5D **26**
Kingie *High* 3C **38**
Kinglassie *Fife* 4D **26**
Kingledores *Bord* 1A **12**
King o' Muirs *Clac* 4H **25**
Kingoodie *Per* 1E **27**
Kingsbarns *Fife* 2G **27**
Kingsburgh *High* 3C **44**
Kingscavil *W Lot* 1F **19**
Kingscross *N Ayr* 1F **9**
Kingseat *Fife* 4C **26**
Kingsford *E Ayr* 4H **17**
Kingshouse *High* 3F **31**
Kingshouse *Stir* 1E **25**
Kingskettle *Fife* 3E **27**
Kingsmuir *Ang* 4B **34**
Kingsmuir *Fife* 3G **27**
Kings Muir *Bord* 5H **19**
Kingsteps *High* 3C **48**
Kingston *E Lot* 5G **27**
Kingston *Mor* 2G **49**
Kingswells *Aber* 3D **42**
Kingswood *Per* 5F **33**
Kingussie *High* 3A **40**
Kinharrachie *Abers* 5E **51**
Kinhrive *High* 1H **47**
Kinkell Bridge *Per* 2A **26**
Kinknockie *Abers* 4F **51**
Kinkry Hill *Cumb* 1H **7**
Kinloch *High*
nr. Lochaline 3H **29**
Kinloch *High*
nr. Loch More 5E **57**
Kinloch *High*
on Rùm 4C **36**
Kinloch *Per* 4G **33**
Kinlochard *Stir* 3D **24**
Kinlochbervie *High* 3D **56**
Kinlocheil *High* 1C **30**
Kinlochewe *High* 2B **46**
Kinloch Hourn *High* 3A **38**
Kinloch Laggan *High* 5G **39**
Kinlochleven *High* 2E **31**
Kinloch Lodge *High* 3G **57**
Kinlochmoidart *High* 1A **30**
Kinlochmore *High* 2E **31**
Kinloch Rannoch *Per* 3B **32**
Kinlochspelve *Arg* 1D **22**
Kinloid *High* 5F **37**

Kinloss—Millikenpark

Kinloss Mor 2D 48
Kinmuck Abers 2D 42
Kinnadie Abers 4E 51
Kinnaird Per 1D 26
Kinneff Abers 1F 35
Kinnelhead Dum 3H 11
Kinnell Ang 3D 34
Kinnernie Abers 3C 42
Kinnesswood Per 3C 26
Kinnordy Ang 3A 34
Kinross Per 3C 26
Kinrossie Per 5G 33
Kintessack Mor 2D 48
Kintillo Per 2C 26
Kintore Abers 2C 42
Kintour Arg 3F 15
Kintra Arg 1A 22
Kintraw Arg 3F 23
Kinveachy High 2C 40
Kippen Stir 4F 25
Kippford Dum 3B 6
Kirbister Orkn
nr. Hobbister 4C 64
Kirbister Orkn
nr. Quholm 3B 64
Kirbuster Orkn 5J 65
Kirk High 3F 59
Kirkabister Shet
on Bressay 3D 66
Kirkabister Shet
on Mainland 1D 66
Kirkandrews Dum 4H 5
Kirkandrews-on-Eden Cumb 3G 7
Kirkapol Arg 4B 28
Kirkbampton Cumb 3G 7
Kirkbean Dum 3C 6
Kirkbride Cumb 3F 7
Kirkbuddo Ang 4C 34
Kirkcaldy Fife **83 (4D 26)**
Kirkcolm Dum 2B 4
Kirkconnel Dum 2E 11
Kirkconnell Dum 2C 6
Kirkcowan Dum 2E 5
Kirkcudbright Dum 3H 5
Kirkfieldbank S Lan 4D 18
Kirkforthar Feus Fife 3D 26
Kirkgunzeon Dum 2B 6
Kirkhill Ang 2D 34
Kirkhill High 4G 47
Kirkhope S Lan 3G 11
Kirkhouse Bord 5A 20
Kirkibost High 2E 37
Kirkinch Ang 4A 34
Kirkinner Dum 3F 5
Kirkintilloch E Dun 1B 18
Kirkland Cumb 4F 7
Kirkland Dum
nr. Kirkconnel 2E 11
Kirkland Dum
nr. Moniaive 4F 11
Kirkland Guards Cumb 4E 7
Kirklauchline Dum 3B 4
Kirklinton Cumb 2H 7
Kirkliston Edin 1G 19
Kirkmabreck Dum 3F 5
Kirkmaiden Dum 5C 4
Kirkmichael Per 2F 33
Kirkmichael S Ayr 3A 10
Kirkmuirhill S Lan 4C 18
Kirknewton Nmbd 5G 21
Kirknewton W Lot 2G 19
Kirkney Abers 5A 50
Kirk of Shotts N Lan 2D 18
Kirkoswald S Ayr 3H 9
Kirkpatrick Dum 4G 11
Kirkpatrick Durham Dum 1A 6
Kirkpatrick-Fleming Dum 1F 7
Kirkstile Dum 4C 12
Kirkstyle High 1G 59
Kirkton Abers
nr. Alford 2B 42
Kirkton Abers
nr. Insch 1B 42
Kirkton Abers
nr. Turriff 4D 50
Kirkton Ang
nr. Dundee 5B 34
Kirkton Ang
nr. Forfar 4B 34
Kirkton Ang
nr. Tarfside 5H 41
Kirkton Dum 5G 11
Kirkton Fife 1E 27
Kirkton High
nr. Golspie 4E 55
Kirkton High
nr. Kyle of Lochalsh 1H 37
Kirkton High
nr. Lochcarron 4A 46
Kirkton Bord 2E 13
Kirkton S Lan 1G 11
Kirktonhill W Dun 1G 17
Kirkton Manor Bord 5H 19
Kirkton of Airlie Ang 3A 34
Kirkton of Auchterhouse
Ang 5A 34
Kirkton of Bourtie Abers 1D 42
Kirkton of Collace Per 5G 33
Kirkton of Craig Ang 3E 35
Kirkton of Culsalmond
Abers 5B 50
Kirkton of Durris Abers 4C 42
Kirkton of Glenbuchat
Abers 2G 41
Kirkton of Glenisla Ang 2H 33
Kirkton of Kingoldrum
Ang 3A 34
Kirkton of Largo Fife 3F 27
Kirkton of Lethendy Per 4G 33
Kirkton of Logie Buchan
Abers 1E 43
Kirkton of Maryculter
Abers 4D 42
Kirkton of Menmuir Ang 2C 34
Kirkton of Monikie Ang 5C 34
Kirkton of Oyne Abers 1B 42
Kirkton of Rayne Abers 5B 50
Kirkton of Skene Abers 3D 42
Kirktown Abers
nr. Fraserburgh 2E 51
Kirktown Abers
nr. Peterhead 3F 51
Kirktown of Alvah Abers 2B 50
Kirktown of Auchterless
Abers 4C 50
Kirktown of Deskford Mor 2A 50
Kirktown of Fetteresso
Abers 5D 42
Kirktown of Mortlach Mor 5G 49
Kirktown of Slains Abers 1F 43
Kirkurd Bord 4G 19
Kirkwall Orkn 3D 64
Kirkwall Airport Orkn 4D 64
Kirk Yetholm Bord 1H 13
Kirn Arg 1E 17
Kirriemuir Ang 3A 34
Kirtlebridge Dum 1F 7
Kirtleton Dum 1F 7
Kirtomy High 2A 58
Kishorn High 4H 45
Kittybrewster Aber 3E 43
Knapp Per 5H 33
Knapperfield High 3F 59
Knaven Abers 4D 50
Knightswood Glas 2A 18
Knock Arg 5G 29
Knock Mor 3A 50
Knockally High 5E 59
Knockan Arg 1B 22
Knockan High 2H 53
Knockandhu Mor 1F 41
Knockando Mor 4E 49
Knockarthur High 3E 55
Knockbain High 3H 47
Knockbreck High 2B 44
Knockdee High 2E 59
Knockdolian S Ayr 5G 9
Knockdon S Ayr 2A 10
Knockenbaird Abers 1B 42
Knockenkelly N Ayr 1F 9
Knockentiber E Ayr 5G 17
Knockfarrel High 3G 47
Knockglass High 2D 58
Knockie Lodge High 2F 39
Knockinlaw E Ayr 5H 17
Knockinnon High 5E 59
Knockrome Arg 1G 15
Knockshinnoch E Ayr 2B 10
Knockvennie Dum 1A 6
Knockvologan Arg 2A 22
Knott High 3C 44
Knowe Dum 1E 5
Knowefield Cumb 3H 7
Knowehead Dum 4D 10
Knowes E Lot 1D 20
Knoweside S Ayr 2H 9
Knowes of Elrick Abers 3B 50
Kyleakin High 1G 37
Kyle of Lochalsh High 1G 37
Kylerhea High 1G 37
Kylesku High 5D 56
Kyles Lodge W Isl 2K 61
Kylesmorar High 4H 37
Kylestrome High 5D 56

L

Labost W Isl 3G 63
Lacasaidh W Isl 2E 62
Lacasdail W Isl 4J 63
Lady Orkn 3J 65
Ladybank Fife 2E 27
Ladykirk Bord 4F 21
Ladysford Abers 2E 51
Laga High 2H 29
Lagavulin Arg 4F 15
Lagg Arg 1G 15
Lagg N Ayr 1E 9
Laggan Arg 3D 14
Laggan High
nr. Fort Augustus 4D 38
Laggan High
nr. Newtonmore 4H 39
Laggan Mor 5G 49
Lagganlia High 3B 40
Lagganulva Arg 4F 29
Laglingarten Arg 3A 24
Laid High 3F 57
Laide High 4D 52
Laigh Fenwick E Ayr 4H 17
Laigh High 3C 54
Lairg Muir High 3C 54
Laithes Cumb 5H 7
Lamancha Bord 3H 19
Lambden Bord 4E 21
Lamberton Bord 3G 21
Lambhill Glas 2A 18
Laminess Orkn 4J 65
Lamington High 1A 48
Lamington S Lan 5E 19
Lamlash N Ayr 5D 16
Lamonby Cumb 5H 7
Lanark S Lan 4D 18
Landerberry Abers 3C 42
Landhallow High 5E 59
Lanehead Nmbd 5G 13
Langais W Isl 4J 61
Langal High 2A 30
Langbank Ren 1G 17
Langburnshiels Bord 3E 13
Langdyke Fife 3E 27
Langholm Dum 5C 12
Langrigg Cumb 4E 7
Langshaw Bord 5C 20
Lanton Nmbd 5G 21
Lanton Bord 1F 13
Laphroaig Arg 4E 15
Larachbeg High 4H 29
Larbert Falk 5H 25
Larel High 3E 59
Largie Abers 5B 50
Largiemore Arg 5G 23
Largoward Fife 3F 27
Largs N Ayr 3F 17
Largue Abers 4B 50
Largybeg N Ayr 1F 9
Largymeanoch N Ayr 1F 9
Largymore N Ayr 1F 9
Larkfield Inv 1F 17
Larkhall S Lan 3C 18
Lary Abers 3G 41
Lasswade Midl 2A 20
Latheron High 5E 59
Latheronwheel High 5E 59
Lathones Fife 3F 27
Laudale House High 3A 30
Lauder Bord 4C 20
Laurencekirk Abers 1E 35
Laurieston Dum 2H 5
Laurieston Falk 1E 19
Lauriston Edin 7E 74
Laverhay Dum 4A 12
Laversdale Cumb 2H 7
Law S Lan 3D 18
Lawers Per 5B 32
Laxfirth Shet 1D 66
Laxo Shet 6H 67
Leac a Li W Isl 5C 62
Leachd Arg 4H 23
Leachkin High 4H 47
Leadburn Midl 3H 19
Leaderfoot Bord 5C 20
Leadhills S Lan 2F 11
Lealt Arg 4D 22
Lealt High 2E 45
Leargybreck Arg 1G 15
Leaths Dum 2A 6
Leckfurin High 3A 58
Leckgruinart Arg 2D 14
Leckmelm High 4G 53
Ledaig Arg 5C 30
Ledgowan High 3C 46
Ledmore High 2H 53
Lednabirichen High 4E 55
Lednagullin High 2B 58
Leeans Shet 2C 66
Leebotten Shet 4D 66
Leetown Per 1D 26
Legerwood Bord 4C 20
Leirinmore High 2F 57
Leishmore High 4F 47
Leitfie Per 4H 33
Leith Edin 1H 19
Leitholm Bord 4E 21
Lempitlaw Bord 5E 21
Lenchie Abers 5A 50
Lendalfoot S Ayr 5G 9
Lendrick Stir 3E 25
Lenimore N Ayr 4B 16
Lennel Bord 4F 21
Lennoxtown E Dun 1B 18
Lentran High 4G 47
Lenzie E Dun 1B 18
Leochel Cushnie Abers 2A 42
Leogh Shet 1J 65
Lephenstrath Arg 3B 8
Lephin High 4A 44
Lephinchapel Arg 4G 23
Lephinmore Arg 4G 23
Lerwick Shet 2D 66
Lerwick (Tingwall) Airport
Shet 2D 66
Leslie Abers 1A 42
Leslie Fife 3D 26
Lesmahagow S Lan 5D 18
Lessonhall Cumb 3F 7
Leswalt Dum 2B 4
Letham Ang 4C 34
Letham Falk 5H 25
Letham Fife 2E 27
Lethanhill E Ayr 2B 10
Lethenty Abers 4D 50
Lettan Orkn 3K 65
Letter Abers 2C 42
Letterewe High 1A 46
Letterfearn High 1H 37
Lettermore Arg 4F 29
Letters High 5G 53
Leuchars Fife 1F 27
Leumrabhagh W Isl 3E 62
Levaneap Shet 6H 67
Leven Fife 3E 27
Levencorroch N Ayr 1F 9
Levenhall E Lot 1A 20
Levenwick Shet 4D 66
Leverburgh W Isl 6B 62
Levishie High 2F 39
Lewiston High 1G 39
Leylodge Abers 2C 42
Leys Per 5H 33
Leysmill Ang 4D 34
Lhanbryde Mor 2F 49
Liatrie High 5D 46
Libberton S Lan 4E 19
Liberton Edin 2H 19
Liceasto W Isl 5C 62
Liddle Orkn 6D 64
Lienassie High 1A 38
Liff Ang 5A 34
Lilliesleaf Bord 1C 12
Lilybank Inv 1G 17
Limekilnburn S Lan 3C 18
Limekilns Fife 5B 26
Limerigg Falk 1D 18
Linburn W Lot 2G 19
Lincluden Dum 1C 6
Lindean Bord 5B 20
Lindores Fife 2D 26
Lingreabhagh W Isl 6B 62
Lingy Close Cumb 3G 7
Linicro High 2C 44
Linklater Orkn 6D 64
Linksness Orkn 3E 64
Linktown Fife 4D 26
Linkwood Mor 2F 49
Linlithgow W Lot 1E 19
Linlithgow Bridge Falk 1E 19
Linneraineach High 3G 53
Linshiels Nmbd 3H 13
Linsiadar W Isl 1D 62
Linsidemore High 4C 54
Linstock Cumb 3H 7
Lintlaw Bord 3F 21
Lintmill Mor 2A 50
Linton Bord 1G 13
Linwood Ren 2H 17
Lionacleit W Isl 6H 61
Lionacro High 2C 44
Lionacuidhe W Isl 6H 61
Lional W Isl 1K 63
Liquo N Lan 3D 18
Litterty Abers 3C 50
Little Ardo Abers 5D 50
Little Ballinluig Per 3E 33
Little Bampton Cumb 3F 7
Little Blencow Cumb 5H 7
Little Brechin Ang 2C 34
Little Broughton Cumb 5D 6
Little Clifton Cumb 5D 6
Little Creich High 5D 54
Little Crosthwaite Cumb 5F 7
Little Dens Abers 4F 51
Little Dunkeld Per 4F 33
Littleferry High 4F 55
Little Glenshee Per 5E 33
Littlemill Abers 4G 41
Littlemill E Ayr 2B 10
Littlemill High 4C 48
Little Orton Cumb 3G 7
Little Rogart High 3E 55
Little Scatwell High 3E 47
Littlester Shet 4J 67
Little Torboll High 4E 55
Littletown High 5E 55
Liurbost W Isl 2E 62
Livingston W Lot 2F 19
Livingston Village W Lot 2F 19
Loan Falk 1E 19
Loanend Nmbd 3G 21
Loanhead Midl 2H 19
Loaningfoot Dum 3C 6
Loanreoch High 1H 47
Loans S Ayr 5G 17
Lochaber Mor 3D 48
Loch a Charnain W Isl 6J 61
Loch a Ghainmhich W Isl 2D 62
Lochailort High 5G 37
Lochaline High 4H 29
Lochans Dum 3B 4
Locharbriggs Dum 5G 11
Lochardil High 4H 47
Lochassynt Lodge High 1G 53
Lochavich Arg 2G 23
Lochawe Arg 1A 24
Loch Baghasdail W Isl 3C 60
Lochboisdale W Isl 3C 60
Lochbuie Arg 1D 22
Lochcarron High 5H 45
Loch Choire Lodge High 5H 57
Lochdochart House Stir 1D 24
Lochdon Arg 5A 30
Lochearnhead Stir 1E 25
Lochee D'dee 5A 34
Lochend High
nr. Inverness 5G 47
Lochend High
nr. Thurso 2F 59
Locherben Dum 4G 11
Loch Euphort W Isl 4J 61
Lochfoot Dum 1B 6
Lochgair Arg 4G 23
Lochgarthside High 2G 39
Lochgelly Fife 4C 26
Lochgilphead Arg 5F 23
Lochgoilhead Arg 3A 24
Loch Head Dum 4E 5
Lochhill Mor 2F 49
Lochindorb Lodge High 5C 48
Lochinver High 1F 53
Lochlane Per 1H 25
Loch Lomond Arg 3C 24
Loch Loyal Lodge High 4H 57
Lochluichart High 2E 47
Lochmaben Dum 5H 11
Lochmaddy W Isl 4K 61
Loch nam Madadh W Isl 4K 61
Lochore Fife 4C 26
Lochportain W Isl 3K 61
Lochranza N Ayr 3C 16
Loch Sgioport W Isl 1D 60
Lochside Abers 2E 35
Lochside High
nr. Achentoul 5B 58
Lochside High
nr. Nairn 3B 48
Lochslin High 5F 55
Lochstack Lodge High 4D 56
Lochton Abers 4C 42
Lochty Fife 3G 27
Lochuisge High 3A 30
Lochussie High 3F 47
Lochwinnoch Ren 3G 17
Lochyside High 1E 31
Lockerbie Dum 5A 12
Lockhills Cumb 4H 7
Logan E Ayr 1C 10
Loganlea W Lot 2E 19
Loggie High 4G 53
Logie Ang 2D 34
Logie Fife 1F 27
Logie Mor 3D 48
Logie Coldstone Abers 3H 41
Logie Pert Ang 2D 34
Logierait Per 3E 33
Lonbain High 3F 45
Londubh High 5D 52
Lone High 4E 57
Lonemore High
nr. Dornoch 5E 55
Lonemore High
nr. Gairloch 1G 45
Longbar N Ayr 3G 17
Longburgh Cumb 3G 7
Longcroft Cumb 3F 7
Longcroft Falk 1C 18
Longdales Cumb 4H 7
Longfield Shet 5C 66
Longforgan Per 5A 34
Longformacus Bord 3D 20
Longhill Abers 3F 51
Longhope Orkn 5C 64
Longlands Cumb 5F 7
Longmanhill Abers 2C 50
Longmorn Mor 3F 49
Longnewton Bord 1E 13
Longniddry E Lot 1B 20
Longpark Cumb 2H 7
Longridge W Lot 2E 19
Longriggend N Lan 1D 18
Longside Abers 4F 51
Longtown Cumb 2G 7
Longyester E Lot 2C 20
Lonmore High 4B 44
Lossiemouth Mor 2F 49
Lossit Arg 3C 14
Lothbeg High 2G 55
Lothianbridge Midl 2A 20
Lothianburn Midl 2H 19
Lothmore High 2G 55
Low Ardwell Dum 4B 4
Low Ballochdowan S Ayr 1B 4
Low Braithwaite Cumb 4H 7
Low Coylton S Ayr 2B 10
Low Crosby Cumb 3H 7
Lower Arboll High 5F 55
Lower Auchenreath Mor 2G 49
Lower Badcall High 4C 56
Lower Breakish High 1F 37
Lower Diabaig High 2G 45
Lower Dounreay High 2C 58
Lower Gledfield High 4C 54
Lower Killeyan Arg 4D 14
Lower Largo Fife 3F 27
Lower Lenie High 1G 39
Lower Milovaig High 3A 44
Lower Oakfield Fife 4C 26
Lower Ollach High 5E 45
Lower Pitkerrie High 1B 48
Lowertown Orkn 5D 64
Low Hesket Cumb 4H 7
Lowick Nmbd 5H 21
Low Lorton Cumb 5E 7
Lownie Moor Ang 4B 34
Lowood Bord 5C 20
Low Row Cumb 4E 7
Low Torry Fife 5B 26
Low Valleyfield Fife 5A 26
Low Whinnow Cumb 3G 7
Lubcroy High 3A 54
Lubinvullin High 2G 57
Lucklawhill Fife 1F 27
Ludag W Isl 3C 60
Lugar E Ayr 1C 10
Luggate Burn E Lot 1D 20
Luggiebank N Lan 1C 18
Lugton E Ayr 3H 17
Luib High 1E 37
Luib Stir 1D 24
Lumphanan Abers 3A 42
Lumphinnans Fife 4C 26
Lumsdaine Bord 2F 21
Lumsden Abers 1H 41
Lunan Ang 3D 34
Lunanhead Ang 3B 34
Luncarty Per 1B 26
Lundie Ang 5H 33
Lundin Links Fife 3F 27
Lunna Shet 6H 67
Lunning Shet 6J 67
Luss Arg 4C 24
Lussagiven Arg 5D 22
Lusta High 3B 44
Luthermuir Abers 2D 34
Luthrie Fife 2E 27
Lybster High 5F 59
Lyham Nmbd 5H 21
Lylestone N Ayr 4G 17
Lynaberack Lodge High 3A 40
Lynchat High 3A 40
Lyne Bord 4H 19
Lyneholmeford Cumb 1H 7
Lyne of Gorthleck High 1G 39
Lyne of Skene Abers 2C 42
Lyness Orkn 5C 64
Lynwilg High 2B 40
Lyth High 2F 59
Lythes Orkn 6D 64
Lythmore High 2D 58

M

Mabie Dum 1C 6
Macbiehill Bord 3G 19
Macduff Abers 2C 50
Machan S Lan 3C 18
Macharioch Arg 3C 8
Machrie N Ayr 5B 16
Machrihanish Arg 1B 8
Macmerry E Lot 1B 20
Madderty Per 1A 26
Maddiston Falk 1E 19
Maggieknockater Mor 4G 49
Maidens S Ayr 3H 9
Mail Shet 4D 66
Mains of Auchindachy Mor 4H 49
Mains of Auchnagatt Abers 4E 51
Mains of Drum Abers 4D 42
Mains of Edingight Mor 3A 50
Mainsriddle Dum 3C 6
Makerstoun Bord 5D 20
Malacleit W Isl 3H 61
Malaig High 4F 37
Malaig Bheag High 4F 37
Malcolmburn Mor 3G 49
Maligar High 2D 44
Mallaig High 4F 37
Malleny Mills Edin 2G 19
Malt Lane Arg 3H 23
Manais W Isl 6C 62
Mangurstadh W Isl 1B 62
Mannal Arg 4A 28
Mannerston Falk 1F 19
Mannofield Aber 3E 43
Mansewood Glas 2A 18
Mansfield E Ayr 2D 10
Maraig W Isl 4D 62
Marbhig W Isl 6J 63
Margnaheglish N Ayr 5D 16
Marishader High 2D 44
Marjoriebanks Dum 5H 11
Mark Dum 3C 4
Markethill Per 5H 33
Markinch Fife 3D 26
Mar Lodge Abers 5D 40
Marnoch Abers 3A 50
Marnock N Lan 2C 18
Marrel High 2H 55
Marrister Shet 6J 67
Marshall Meadows Nmbd 3G 21
Marwick Orkn 2B 64
Marybank High
nr. Dingwall 3F 47
Marybank High
nr. Invergordon 1A 48
Maryburgh High 3G 47
Maryhill Glas 2A 18
Marykirk Abers 2D 34
Marypark Mor 5E 49
Maryport Cumb 5D 6
Maryport Dum 5C 4
Maryton Ang
nr. Kirriemuir 3A 34
Maryton Ang
nr. Montrose 3D 34
Marywell Abers 4A 42
Marywell Ang 4D 34
Masons Lodge Abers 3D 42
Mastrick Aber 3E 43
Mauchline E Ayr 1B 10
Maud Abers 4E 51
Mawbray Cumb 4D 6
Maxton Bord 5D 20
Maxwellheugh Bord 5E 21
Maxwelltown Dum 1C 6
Maybole S Ayr 3A 10
Mayfield Midl 2A 20
Mayfield Per 1B 26
Maywick Shet 4C 66
Meadowmill E Lot 1B 20
Mealabost W Isl
nr. Borgh 2J 63
Mealabost W Isl
nr. Stornoway 4J 63
Mealasta W Isl 2A 62
Mealrigg Cumb 4E 7
Mealsgate Cumb 4F 7
Meigle Per 4H 33
Meikle Earnock S Lan 3C 18
Meikle Kilchattan Butts
Arg 3D 16
Meikleour Per 5G 33
Meikle Tarty Abers 1E 43
Meikle Wartle Abers 5C 50
Melby Shet 1A 66
Melfort Arg 2F 23
Melgarve High 4F 39
Melkington Nmbd 4F 21
Mellangaun High 5D 52
Melldalloch Arg 1C 16
Mellguards Cumb 4H 7
Mellon Charles High 4D 52
Mellon Udrigle High 4D 52
Melrose Bord 5C 20
Melsetter Orkn 6B 64
Melvaig High 5C 52
Melvich High 2B 58
Memsie Abers 2E 51
Memus Ang 3B 34
Mennock Dum 3F 11
Menstrie Clac 4H 25
Merchiston Edin 1H 19
Merkadale High 5C 44
Merkland S Ayr 4H 9
Merkland Lodge High 1A 54
Methil Fife 4E 27
Methilhill Fife 4E 27
Methlick Abers 5D 50
Methven Per 1B 26
Mey High 1F 59
Miabhag W Isl 5C 62
Miabhaig W Isl
nr. Cliasmol 4B 62
Miabhaig W Isl
nr. Timsgearraidh 1B 62
Mial High 1G 45
Micklethwaite Cumb 3F 7
Mid Ardlaw Abers 2E 51
Midbea Orkn 3G 65
Mid Beltie Abers 3B 42
Mid Calder W Lot 2F 19
Mid Clyth High 5F 59
Middlebie Dum 1F 7
Middle Drums Ang 3C 34
Middle Essie Abers 3F 51
Middlemuir Abers
nr. New Deer 4D 50
Middlemuir Abers
nr. Strichen 3E 51
Middlesceugh Cumb 4G 7
Middleton Ang 4C 34
Middleton Arg 4A 28
Middleton Midl 3A 20
Middleton Nmbd 5H 21
Middleton Per 3C 26
Midfield High 2G 57
Mid Garrary Dum 1G 5
Mid Ho Shet 3J 67
Mid Kirkton N Ayr 3E 17
Midland Orkn 4C 64
Midlem Bord 1E 13
Midton Inv 1F 17
Midtown High
nr. Poolewe 5D 52
Midtown High
nr. Tongue 2G 57
Mid Walls Shet 2A 66
Mid Yell Shet 3J 67
Migdale High 4D 54
Migvie Abers 3H 41
Milesmark Fife 5B 26
Milfield Nmbd 5G 21
Millbank High 2E 59
Millbeck Cumb 5F 7
Millbounds Orkn 1E 64
Millbreck Abers 4F 51
Millden Lodge Ang 1C 34
Milldens Ang 3C 34
Millearn Per 2A 26
Millerhill Midl 2A 20
Millerston Glas 2B 18
Millfield Abers 4H 41
Millhall E Ren 3A 18
Millheugh S Lan 3C 18
Millhouse Arg 1C 16
Millhouse Cumb 5G 7
Millhousebridge Dum 5A 12
Millikenpark Ren 2H 17

Mill Knowe—Prospect

Mill Knowe *Arg* 1C 8
Mill of Craigievar *Abers* 2A 42
Mill of Fintray *Abers* 2D 42
Mill of Haldane *W Dun* 5D 24
Millport *N Ayr* 3E 17
Milltimber *Aber* 3D 42
Milltown *Abers*
nr. Corgarff 3F 41
Milltown *Abers*
nr. Lumsden 2H 41
Milltown *Dum* 1G 7
Milltown of Aberdalgie
Per 1B 26
Milltown of Auchindoun
Mor 4G 49
Milltown of Campfield
Abers 3B 42
Milltown of Edinvillie *Mor* 4F 49
Milltown of Rothiemay
Mor 4A 50
Milltown of Towie *Abers* 2H 41
Milnacraig *Ang* 3H 33
Milnathort *Per* 3C 26
Milngavie *E Dun* 1A 18
Milnholm *Stir* 5G 25
Milton *Ang* 4A 34
Milton *Dum*
nr. Crocketford 1B 6
Milton *Dum*
nr. Glenluce 3D 4
Milton *Glas* 2A 18
Milton *High*
nr. Achnasheen 3E 47
Milton *High*
nr. Applecross 4G 45
Milton *High*
nr. Drumnadrochit 5F 47
Milton *High*
nr. Invergordon 1A 48
Milton *High*
nr. Inverness 4G 47
Milton *High*
nr. Wick 3G 59
Milton *Mor*
nr. Cullen 2A 50
Milton *Mor*
nr. Tomintoul 2E 41
Milton *S Ayr* 1B 10
Milton *Stir*
nr. Aberfoyle 3E 25
Milton *Stir*
nr. Drymen 4D 24
Milton *W Dun* 1H 17
Milton Auchlossan *Abers* 3A 42
Milton Bridge *Midl* 2H 19
Milton Coldwells *Abers* 5E 51
Miltonduff *Mor* 2E 49
Milton Morenish *Per* 5B 32
Milton of Auchinhove
Abers 3A 42
Milton of Balgonie *Fife* 3E 27
Milton of Barras *Abers* 1F 35
Milton of Campsie *E Dun* 1B 18
Milton of Cultoquhey *Per* 1H 25
Milton of Cushnie *Abers* 2A 42
Milton of Finavon *Ang* 3B 34
Milton of Gollanfield *High* 3A 48
Milton of Lesmore *Abers* 1H 41
Milton of Leys *High* 4H 47
Milton of Tullich *Abers* 4G 41
Minard *Arg* 4G 23
Mindrum *Nmbd* 5F 21
Mingarrypark *High* 2H 29
Mingary *High* 2G 29
Mingearraidh *W Isl* 2C 60
Minishant *S Ayr* 2A 10
Minnigaff *Dum* 2F 5
Mintlaw *Abers* 4F 51
Minto *Bord* 1E 13
Miodar *Arg* 4B 28
Mirbister *Orkn* 2C 64
Mireland *High* 2G 59
Moaness *Orkn* 4B 64
Moarfield *Shet* 2J 67
Moat *Cumb* 1H 7
Mochrum *Dum* 4E 5
Modsarie *High* 2H 57
Moffat *Dum* 3H 11
Mol-chlach *High* 2D 36
Moll *High* 1E 37
Mollinsburn *N Lan* 1C 18
Monachyle *Stir* 2D 24
Monar Lodge *High* 4D 46
Moneydie *Per* 1B 26
Moniaive *Dum* 4E 11
Monifieth *Ang* 5C 34
Monikie *Ang* 5C 34
Monimail *Fife* 2D 26
Monkhill *Cumb* 3G 7
Monkshill *Abers* 4C 50
Monkton *S Ayr* 1A 10
Monktonhill *S Ayr* 1A 10
Monreith *Dum* 4E 5
Montford *Arg* 2E 17
Montgarrie *Abers* 2A 42
Montgarswood *E Ayr* 1C 10
Montgreenan *N Ayr* 4G 17
Montrave *Fife* 3E 27
Montrose *Ang* 3E 35
Monymusk *Abers* 2B 42
Monzie *Per* 1H 25
Moodiesburn *N Lan* 1B 18
Moonzie *Fife* 2E 27
Moorbrae *Shet* 4H 67
Moorend *Dum* 1F 7
Moorhouse *Cumb*
nr. Carlisle 3G 7
Moorhouse *Cumb*
nr. Wigton 3F 7
Moor of Granary *Mor* 3D 48
Moor Row *Cumb* 4F 7
Morangie *High* 5E 55
Morar *High* 4F 37
Morebattle *Bord* 1G 13
Morefield *High* 4G 53
Morenish *Per* 5A 32
Morham *E Lot* 1C 20
Morningside *Edin* 1H 19
Morningside *N Lan* 3D 18
Morrington *Dum* 5F 11
Morton *Cumb*
nr. Calthwaite 5H 7
Morton *Cumb*
nr. Carlisle 3G 7
Morvich *High*
nr. Golspie 3E 55
Morvich *High*
nr. Shiel Bridge 1A 38
Moscow *E Ayr* 4H 17
Mosedale *Cumb* 5G 7
Moss *Arg* 4A 28
Moss *High* 2H 29
Mossatt *Abers* 2H 41
Mossbank *Shet* 5H 67
Mossblown *S Ayr* 1B 10
Mossburnford *Bord* 2F 13
Mossdale *Dum* 1H 5
Mossedge *Cumb* 2H 7
Mossend *N Lan* 2C 18
Moss of Barmuckity *Mor* 2F 49
Mosspark *Glas* 2A 18
Mosspaul *Bord* 4D 12
Moss Side *Cumb* 3E 7
Moss-side *High* 3B 48
Moss-side of Cairness
Abers 2F 51
Mosstodloch *Mor* 2G 49
Motherby *Cumb* 5H 7
Motherwell *N Lan* 84 (3C 18)
Moulin *Per* 3E 33
Mountain Cross *Bord* 4G 19
Mountbenger *Bord* 1C 12
Mountblow *W Dun* 1H 17
Mountgerald *High* 2G 47
Mount High *High* 2H 47
Mount Lothian *Midl* 3H 19
Mount Stuart *Arg* 3E 17
Mouswald *Dum* 1D 6
Mowhaugh *Bord* 1H 13
Moy *High* 5A 48
Moy Lodge *High* 5F 39
Muasdale *Arg* 4H 15
Muchalls *Abers* 4E 43
Muchrachd *High* 5D 46
Muckle Breck *Shet* 6J 67
Mudale *High* 5G 57
Mugdock *Stir* 1A 18
Mugeary *High* 5D 44
Muie *High* 3D 54
Muirden *Abers* 3C 50
Muirdrum *Ang* 5C 34
Muiredge *Per* 1D 26
Muirend *Glas* 2A 18
Muirhead *Ang* 5A 34
Muirhead *Fife* 3D 26
Muirhead *N Lan* 2B 18
Muirhouses *Falk* 5B 26
Muirkirk *E Ayr* 1D 10
Muir of Alford *Abers* 2A 42
Muir of Fairburn *High* 3F 47
Muir of Fowlis *Abers* 2A 42
Muir of Miltonduff *Mor* 3E 49
Muir of Ord *High* 3G 47
Muir of Tarradale *High* 3G 47
Muirshearlich *High* 5C 38
Muirtack *Abers* 5E 51
Muirton *High* 2A 48
Muirton *Per* 1C 26
Muirton of Ardblair *Per* 4G 33
Muirtown *Per* 2A 26
Muiryfold *Abers* 3C 50
Mulben *Mor* 3G 49
Mulindry *Arg* 3E 15
Mulla *Shet* 6H 67
Mullach Charlabhaigh
W Isl 3G 63
Munerigie *High* 3D 38
Muness *Shet* 2K 67
Mungasdale *High* 4E 53
Mungrisdale *Cumb* 5G 7
Munlochy *High* 3H 47
Murieston *W Lot* 2F 19
Murkle *High* 2E 59
Murlaggan *High* 4B 38
Murra *Orkn* 4B 64
The Murray *S Lan* 3B 18
Murrayfield *Edin* 1H 19
Murroes *Ang* 5B 34
Murthly *Per* 5F 33
Murton *Nmbd* 4G 21
Musselburgh *E Lot* 1A 20
Mutehill *Dum* 4H 5
Muthill *Per* 2H 25
Mybster *High* 3E 59
Myrebird *Abers* 4C 42
Myrelandhorn *High* 3F 59

N

Naast *High* 5D 52
Na Buirgh *W Isl* 5B 62
Na Gearrannan *W Isl* 3F 63
Nairn *High* 3B 48
Navidale *High* 2H 55
Nealhouse *Cumb* 3G 7
Nedd *High* 5C 56
Neilston *E Ren* 3H 17
Nemphlar *S Lan* 4D 18
Nenthorn *Bord* 5D 20
Neribus *Arg* 3D 14
Nerston *S Lan* 3B 18
Nesbit *Nmbd* 5G 21
Ness of Tenston *Orkn* 3B 64
Nethanfoot *S Lan* 4D 18
Nether Blainslie *Bord* 4C 20
Netherbrae *Abers* 3C 50
Netherbrough *Orkn* 3C 64
Netherburn *S Lan* 4D 18
Netherby *Cumb* 1G 7
Nether Careston *Ang* 3C 34
Nether Dallachy *Mor* 2G 49
Nether Durdie *Per* 1D 26
Nether Howcleugh *S Lan* 2H 11
Nether Kinmundy *Abers* 4F 51
Netherlaw *Dum* 4A 6
Netherley *Abers* 4D 42
Nethermill *Dum* 5H 11
Nethermills *Mor* 3A 50
Netherplace *E Ren* 3A 18
Netherthird *E Ayr* 2C 10
Netherton *Ang* 3C 34
Netherton *Cumb* 5D 6
Netherton *N Lan* 3C 18
Netherton *Per* 3G 33
Netherton *Stir* 1A 18
Nethertown *High* 1G 59
Nether Urquhart *Fife* 3C 26
Nether Welton *Cumb* 4G 7
Nethy Bridge *High* 1D 40
The Neuk *Abers* 4C 42
New Abbey *Dum* 2C 6
New Aberdour *Abers* 2D 50
New Alyth *Per* 4H 33
Newark *Orkn* 3K 65
Newarthill *N Lan* 3C 18
Newbattle *Midl* 2A 20
Newbie *Dum* 2E 7
Newbiggin *Cumb* 5H 7
Newbigging *Ang*
nr. Monikie 5B 34
Newbigging *Ang*
nr. Newtyle 4H 33
Newbigging *Ang*
nr. Tealing 5B 34
Newbigging *Edin* 1G 19
Newbigging *S Lan* 4F 19
New Bridge *Dum* 1C 6
Newbridge *Edin* 1G 19
Newburgh *Abers* 1E 43
Newburgh *Fife* 2D 26
Newby East *Cumb* 3H 7
New Byth *Abers* 3D 50
Newby West *Cumb* 3G 7
Newcastleton *Bord* 5D 12
New Cowper *Cumb* 4E 7
Newcraighall *Edin* 1A 20
New Cumnock *E Ayr* 2D 10
New Deer *Abers* 4D 50
New Elgin *Mor* 2F 49
New Galloway *Dum* 1H 5
Newhaven *Edin* 1H 19
Newhouse *N Lan* 2C 18
Newington *Edin* 1H 19
New Kelso *High* 4A 46
New Lanark *S Lan* 4D 18
Newlandrig *Midl* 2A 20
Newlands *Cumb* 5G 7
Newlands *High* 4A 48
Newlands of Geise *High* 2D 58
Newlands of Tynet *Mor* 2G 49
New Langholm *Dum* 5C 12
New Leeds *Abers* 3E 51
Newlot *Orkn* 3E 64
New Luce *Dum* 2C 4
Newmachar *Abers* 2D 42
Newmains *N Lan* 3D 18
New Mains of Ury *Abers* 5D 42
Newmarket *W Isl* 4J 63
New Mill *Abers* 4C 50
Newmill *Mor* 3H 49
Newmill *Bord* 2D 12
Newmills *Fife* 5B 26
Newmills *High* 2H 47
Newmiln *Per* 5G 33
Newmilns *E Ayr* 5A 18
Newmore *High*
nr. Dingwall 3G 47
Newmore *High*
nr. Invergordon 1H 47
Newpark *Fife* 2F 27
New Pitsligo *Abers* 3D 50
Newport-on-Tay *Fife* 1F 27
New Prestwick *S Ayr* 1A 10
New Rent *Cumb* 5H 7
New Sauchie *Clac* 4H 25
Newseat *Abers* 5C 50
Newstead *Bord* 5C 20
New Stevenston *N Lan* 3C 18
Newton *Arg* 4H 23
Newton *Dum*
nr. Annan 1F 7
Newton *Dum*
nr. Moffat 4A 12
Newton *High*
nr. Cromarty 2A 48
Newton *High*
nr. Inverness 4A 48
Newton *High*
nr. Kylestrome 5D 56
Newton *High*
nr. Wick 4G 59
Newton *Mor* 2E 49
Newton *Bord* 1F 13
Newton *Shet* 3C 66
Newton *S Lan*
nr. Glasgow 2B 18
Newton *S Lan*
nr. Lanark 5E 19
Newton *W Lot* 1F 19
Newtonairds *Dum* 5F 11
Newton Arlosh *Cumb* 3F 7
Newtongrange *Midl* 2A 20
Newtonhill *Abers* 4E 43
Newtonhill *High* 4G 47
Newton Mearns *E Ren* 3A 18
Newtonmore *High* 4A 40
Newton of Ardtoe *High* 1H 29
Newton of Balcanquhal *Per* 2C 26
Newton of Beltrees *Ren* 3G 17
Newton of Falkland *Fife* 3D 26
Newton of Mountblairy
Abers 3B 50
Newton of Pitcairns *Per* 2B 26
Newton Reigny *Cumb* 5H 7
Newton Rigg *Cumb* 5H 7
Newton Stewart *Dum* 2F 5
Newton upon Ayr *S Ayr* 1A 10
Newtown *Abers* 2C 50
Newtown *Cumb*
nr. Aspatria 4D 6
Newtown *Cumb*
nr. Brampton 2H 7
New Town *E Lot* 1B 20
New Town *Edin* 2D 74
Newtown *Falk* 5A 26
Newtown *High* 3E 39
Newtown *Nmbd* 5H 21
Newtown *Shet* 4H 67
Newtown St Boswells *Bord* 5C 20
Newtyle *Ang* 4H 33
New Winton *E Lot* 1B 20
Niddrie *Edin* 1A 20
Niddry *W Lot* 1F 19
Nigg *Aber* 3E 43
Nigg *High* 1B 48
Nigg Ferry *High* 2A 48
Ninemile Bar *Dum* 1B 6
Nine Mile Burn *Midl* 3G 19
Nisbet *Bord* 1F 13
Nisbet Hill *Bord* 3E 21
Nitshill *Glas* 2A 18
Noness *Shet* 4D 66
Nonikiln *High* 1H 47
Nook *Cumb* 1H 7
Noranside *Ang* 2B 34
Norby *Shet* 1A 66
Norham *Nmbd* 4G 21
North Balfern *Dum* 3F 5
North Ballachulish *High* 2D 30
North Berwick *E Lot* 5G 27
North Collafirth *Shet* 4G 67
North Commonty *Abers* 4D 50
North Craigo *Ang* 2D 34
North Dronley *Ang* 5A 34
Northdyke *Orkn* 2B 64
North Erradale *High* 5C 52
North Fearns *High* 5E 45
North Feorline *N Ayr* 1E 9
Northfield *Aber* 3D 42
North Gluss *Shet* 5G 67
North Hazelrigg *Nmbd* 5H 21
North Kessock *High* 4H 47
North Middleton *Midl* 3A 20
Northmuir *Ang* 3A 34
North Murie *Per* 1D 26
North Ness *Orkn* 5C 64
North Port *Arg* 1H 23
North Queensferry *Fife* 5C 26
North Roe *Shet* 4G 67
North Ronaldsay Airport
Orkn 2K 65
North Row *Cumb* 5F 7
North Sannox *N Ayr* 4D 16
North Shian *Arg* 4C 30
North Side *Cumb* 5D 6
Northtown *Orkn* 5D 64
North Town *Shet* 5C 66
Northwall *Orkn* 3K 65
North Water Bridge *Ang* 2D 34
North Watten *High* 3F 59
North Yardhope *Nmbd* 3H 13
Norton Park *Edin* 2L 75
Norwick *Shet* 1K 67
Noss *Shet* 5C 66
Nostie *High* 1H 37
Nunclose *Cumb* 4H 7
Nunnerie *S Lan* 2G 11
Nybster *High* 2G 59

O

Oakbank *Arg* 5A 30
Oakbank *W Lot* 2F 19
Oakley *Fife* 5B 26
Oakshaw Ford *Cumb* 1H 7
Oape *High* 3B 54
Oathlaw *Ang* 3B 34
Oban *Arg* 84 (1F 23)
Oban *W Isl* 4C 62
Obsdale *High* 2H 47
Ochiltree *E Ayr* 1C 10
Ochtermuthill *Per* 2H 25
Ochtertyre *Per* 1H 25
Ockle *High* 1G 29
Octofad *Arg* 3D 14
Octomore *Arg* 3D 14
Oddsta *Shet* 3J 67
Odie *Orkn* 5J 65
Okraquoy *Shet* 3D 66
Old Aberdeen *Aber* 3E 43
Oldany *High* 5C 56
Old Blair *Per* 2D 32
Old Bridge of Tilt *Per* 2D 32
Old Bridge of Urr *Dum* 2A 6
Old Dailly *S Ayr* 4H 9
Old Deer *Abers* 4E 51
Old Graitney *Dum* 2G 7
Oldhall *High* 3F 59
Oldhamstocks *E Lot* 1E 21
Old Kilpatrick *W Dun* 1H 17
Old Kinnernie *Abers* 3C 42
Oldmeldrum *Abers* 1D 42
Old Monkland *N Lan* 2C 18
Old Pentland *Midl* 2H 19
Old Philpstoun *W Lot* 1F 19
Old Rayne *Abers* 1B 42
Old Scone *Per* 1C 26
Oldshore Beg *High* 3C 56
Oldshoremore *High* 3D 56
Old Town *Cumb* 4H 7
Old Town *Edin* 6F 74
Oldtown *High* 5C 54
Old Town *Nmbd* 4H 13
Oldwall *Cumb* 2H 7
Old Westhall *Abers* 1B 42
Oldwhat *Abers* 3D 50
Olgrinmore *High* 3D 58
Ollaberry *Shet* 4G 67
Olrig *High* 2E 59
Omunsgarth *Shet* 2C 66
Onich *High* 2D 30
Onthank *E Ayr* 5H 17
Opinan *High*
nr. Gairloch 1G 45
Opinan *High*
nr. Laide 4D 52
Orasaigh *W Isl* 3E 62
Orbost *High* 4B 44
Ord *High* 2F 37
Ordale *Shet* 2K 67
Ordhead *Abers* 2B 42
Ordie *Abers* 3H 41
Ordiquish *Mor* 3G 49
Orgil *Orkn* 4B 64
Ormacleit *W Isl* 1C 60
Ormathwaite *Cumb* 5F 7
Ormiscaig *High* 4D 52
Ormiston *E Lot* 2B 20
Ormsaigbeg *High* 2F 29
Ormsaigmore *High* 2F 29
Ormsary *Arg* 1A 16
Orphir *Orkn* 4C 64
Orthwaite *Cumb* 5F 7
Orton *Mor* 3G 49
Osclay *High* 5F 59
Ose *High* 4C 44
Oskaig *High* 5E 45
Oskamull *Arg* 5F 29
Osmondwall *Orkn* 6C 64
Osnaburgh *Fife* 2F 27
Ospisdale *High* 5E 55
Otterburn *Nmbd* 4H 13
Otterburn Camp *Nmbd* 4H 13
Otterburn Hall *Nmbd* 4H 13
Otter Ferry *Arg* 5G 23
Otterswick *Shet* 4J 67
Oughterby *Cumb* 3F 7
Oughterside *Cumb* 4E 7
Oulton *Cumb* 3F 7
Ousdale *High* 2H 55
Outertown *Orkn* 3B 64
Overbister *Orkn* 3J 65
Over Finlarg *Ang* 4B 34
Overscaig *High* 1B 54
Overton *Aber* 2D 42
Overton *High* 5F 59
Overtown *N Lan* 3D 18
Oxgangs *Edin* 2H 19
Oxnam *Bord* 2G 13
Oxton *Bord* 3B 20
Oykel Bridge *High* 3A 54
Oyne *Abers* 1B 42

P

Pabail Iarach *W Isl* 4K 63
Pabail Uarach *W Isl* 4K 63
Padanaram *Ang* 3B 34
Paddockhole *Dum* 5B 12
Paibeil *W Isl*
on North Uist 4H 61
Paibeil *W Isl*
on Taransay 5B 62
Paiblesgearraidh *W Isl* 4H 61
Pairc Shiaboist *W Isl* 3G 63
Paisley *Ren* 85 (2H 17)
Palgowan *Dum* 5A 10
Palnackie *Dum* 3B 6
Palnure *Dum* 2F 5
Panbride *Ang* 5C 34
Pannanich *Abers* 4G 41
Papa Stour Airport *Shet* 1A 66
Papa Westray Airport
Orkn 2G 65
Papcastle *Cumb* 5E 7
Papigoe *High* 3G 59
Papil *Shet* 3C 66
Papple *E Lot* 1C 20
Park *Abers* 4C 42
Park *Arg* 4C 30
Park *Dum* 4G 11
Parkburn *Abers* 5C 50
Park End *Nmbd* 5H 13
Parkgate *Cumb* 4F 7
Parkgate *Dum* 5H 11
Parkhall *W Dun* 1H 17
Parkhead *Cumb* 4G 7
Parkhead *Glas* 2B 18
Parkneuk *Abers* 1E 35
Parkside *N Lan* 3D 18
Parsonby *Cumb* 5E 7
Partick *Glas* 2A 18
Parton *Cumb* 3F 7
Parton *Dum* 1H 5
Pathhead *Abers* 2E 35
Pathhead *E Ayr* 2D 10
Pathhead *Fife* 4D 26
Pathhead *Midl* 2A 20
Path of Condie *Per* 2B 26
Pathstruie *Per* 2B 26
Patna *E Ayr* 2B 10
Pattiesmuir *Fife* 5B 26
Pawston *Nmbd* 5F 21
Paxton *Bord* 3G 21
Pearsie *Ang* 3A 34
Peaston *E Lot* 2B 20
Peastonbank *E Lot* 2B 20
Peathill *Abers* 2E 51
Peat Inn *Fife* 3F 27
Peaton *Arg* 5B 24
Peebles *Bord* 4H 19
Peel *Bord* 5B 20
Peinchorran *High* 5E 45
Peinlich *High* 3D 44
Pelutho *Cumb* 4E 7
Pencaitland *E Lot* 2B 20
Penicuik *Midl* 2H 19
Penifiler *High* 4D 44
Peninver *Arg* 1C 8
Penkill *S Ayr* 4H 9
Pennan *Abers* 2D 50
Pennyghael *Arg* 1C 22
Pennyvenie *E Ayr* 3B 10
Penpont *Dum* 4F 11
Penrith *Cumb* 5H 7
Penruddock *Cumb* 5H 7
Penston *E Lot* 1B 20
Perceton *N Ayr* 4G 17
Percyhorner *Abers* 2E 51
Perth *Per* 85 (1C 26)
Peterburn *High* 5C 52
Peterculter *Aber* 3D 42
Peterhead *Abers* 4G 51
Petertown *Orkn* 4C 64
Pettinain *S Lan* 4E 19
Pettycur *Fife* 5D 26
Philiphaugh *Bord* 1D 12
Philpstoun *W Lot* 1F 19
Pickletillem *Fife* 1F 27
Pierowall *Orkn* 3G 65
Pilton *Edin* 1H 19
Pinkerton *E Lot* 1E 21
Pinmore *S Ayr* 4H 9
Pinwherry *S Ayr* 5G 9
Piperhill *High* 3B 48
Pirnmill *N Ayr* 4B 16
Pisgah *Stir* 3G 25
Pitagowan *Per* 2D 32
Pitcairn *Per* 3D 32
Pitcairngreen *Per* 1B 26
Pitcalnie *High* 1B 48
Pitcaple *Abers* 1C 42
Pitcox *E Lot* 1D 20
Pitcur *Per* 5H 33
Pitfichie *Abers* 2B 42
Pitgrudy *High* 4E 55
Pitkennedy *Ang* 3C 34
Pitlessie *Fife* 3E 27
Pitlochry *Per* 3E 33
Pitmachie *Abers* 1B 42
Pitmaduthy *High* 1A 48
Pitmedden *Abers* 1D 42
Pitnacree *Per* 3E 33
Pitroddie *Per* 1D 26
Pitscottie *Fife* 2F 27
Pittentrail *High* 3E 55
Pittenweem *Fife* 3G 27
Pittulie *Abers* 2E 51
Pitversie *Per* 2C 26
Plaidy *Abers* 3C 50
Plains *N Lan* 2C 18
Plean *Stir* 5H 25
Plockton *High* 5H 45
Plocrapol *W Isl* 5C 62
Plumbland *Cumb* 5E 7
Plumpton *Cumb* 5H 7
Plumpton Foot *Cumb* 5H 7
Polbae *Dum* 1D 4
Polbain *High* 3F 53
Polbeth *W Lot* 2F 19
Polchar *High* 3B 40
Poles *High* 4E 55
Polglass *High* 3F 53
Polio *High* 1A 48
Polla *High* 3E 57
Polloch *High* 2A 30
Pollok *Glas* 2A 18
Pollokshaws *Glas* 2A 18
Pollokshields *Glas* 2A 18
Polmaily *High* 5F 47
Polmont *Falk* 1E 19
Polnessan *E Ayr* 2B 10
Polnish *High* 5G 37
Polskeoch *Dum* 3D 10
Polton *Midl* 2H 19
Polwarth *Bord* 3E 21
Ponton *Shet* 1C 66
Poolewe *High* 5D 52
Pool o' Muckhart *Clac* 3B 26
Porin *High* 3E 47
Portachoillan *Arg* 3A 16
Port Adhair Bheinn na Faoghla
W Isl 5H 61
Port Adhair Thirlodh *Arg* 4B 28
Port Ann *Arg* 5G 23
Port Appin *Arg* 4C 30
Port Asgaig *Arg* 2F 15
Port Askaig *Arg* 2F 15
Portavadie *Arg* 2C 16
Port Bannatyne *Arg* 2D 16
Port Carlisle *Cumb* 2F 7
Port Charlotte *Arg* 3D 14
Port Driseach *Arg* 1C 16
Port Dundas *Glas* 2A 18
Port Ellen *Arg* 4E 15
Port Elphinstone *Abers* 1C 42
Portencalzie *Dum* 1B 4
Portencross *N Ayr* 4E 17
Port Erroll *Abers* 5F 51
Portessie *Mor* 2H 49
Port Glasgow *Inv* 1G 17
Portgordon *Mor* 2G 49
Portgower *High* 2H 55
Port Henderson *High* 1G 45
Portincaple *Arg* 4B 24
Portinnisherrich *Arg* 2G 23
Portknockie *Mor* 2H 49
Port Lamont *Arg* 1D 16
Portlethen *Abers* 4E 43
Portlethen Village *Abers* 4E 43
Portling *Dum* 3B 6
Port Logan *Dum* 4B 4
Portmahomack *High* 5G 55
Port Mholair *W Isl* 4K 63
Port Mor *High* 1F 29
Portnacroish *Arg* 4C 30
Portnahaven *Arg* 3C 14
Portnalong *High* 5C 44
Portnaluchaig *High* 5F 37
Portnancon *High* 2F 57
Port Nan Giuran *W Isl* 4K 63
Port nan Long *W Isl* 3J 61
Port Nis *W Isl* 1K 63
Portobello *Edin* 1A 20
Port of Menteith *Stir* 3E 25
Portormin *High* 5E 59
Portpatrick *Dum* 3B 4
Port Ramsay *Arg* 4B 30
Portree *High* 4D 44
Port Righ *High* 4D 44
Port Seton *E Lot* 1B 20
Portskerra *High* 2B 58
Portsonachan *Arg* 1H 23
Portsoy *Abers* 2A 50
Porttannachy *Mor* 2G 49
Portuairk *High* 2F 29
Port Wemyss *Arg* 3C 14
Port William *Dum* 4E 5
Potarch *Abers* 4B 42
Potterton *Abers* 2E 43
Poundland *S Ayr* 5G 9
Powfoot *Dum* 2E 7
Powmill *Per* 4B 26
Pressen *Nmbd* 5F 21
Preston *E Lot*
nr. East Linton 1C 20
Preston *E Lot*
nr. Prestonpans 1A 20
Preston *Bord* 3E 21
Prestonmill *Dum* 3C 6
Prestonpans *E Lot* 1A 20
Prestwick *S Ayr* 1A 10
Priesthill *Glas* 2A 18
Priestland *E Ayr* 5A 18
Primsidemill *Bord* 1H 13
Prior Muir *Fife* 2G 27
Prospect *Cumb* 4E 7

HOW TO USE THE PLACES OF INTEREST INDEX

The index reference is to the square in which the symbol (or its pointer) appears; the text may be in a different square; e.g. Braemar Castle . . . . 4E 41 is to be found in square 4E on page 41.

Entries shown without an index reference have the name of the appropriate town plan and its page number; e.g. Aberdeen Cathedral . . . . Aberdeen 69.
For reasons of clarity, these places of interest do not appear on the main map pages.

Terms such as 'museum' etc. are omitted from the text on the map; a key to the various map symbols used can be found on page 2 in the reference.
Any category in the index that does not have its own symbol in the reference will be depicted by a dot.

Entries in italics are not named on the map but are shown with a symbol.
For this type of entry, the nearest village or town name is given, where that name is not already included in the name of the place of interest.

Opening times for places of interest vary considerably depending on the season, day of week or the ownership of the property.
Please check with the nearest Tourist or Visit Scotland Information Centre listed below before starting your journey.

NTS, National Trust for Scotland Property - Always open. NTS, National Trust for Scotland Property - Restricted opening. HS, Historic Scotland.
NP, National Park Property - Always open. NP, National Park Property - Restricted opening.

A

- Abbotsford (summer only) . . . 5C 20
- Aberdeen Art Gallery . . . Aberdeen 69
- Aberdeen Arts Centre & Theatre . . . Aberdeen 69
- Aberdeen Maritime Museum . . . Aberdeen 69
- Aberdeen St Andrew's Episcopal Cathedral . . . Aberdeen 69
- *Aberdeen St Machar's Cathedral* . . . 3E 43
- Aberdeen St Mary's RC Cathedral . . . Aberdeen 69
- Aberdeenshire Farming Museum . . . 4E 51
- Aberdeen Tolbooth Museum . . . Aberdeen 69
- *Aberdeen Visit Scotland Information Centre* - 01224 269180 . . . Aberdeen 69
- *Aberdour Castle* HS . . . 5C 26
- *Aberfeldy Visit Scotland Information Centre* - 01887 820276 . . . 4D 32
- *Aberfoyle Visit Scotland Information Centre* - 01877 381221 . . . 3E 25
- Aberlemno Sculptured Stones HS . . . 3C 34
- Aberlour Distillery . . . 4F 49
- Abernethy Round Tower HS (summer only) . . . 2C 26
- Abhainn Dearg Distillery . . . 1B 62
- Abriachan Garden . . . 5G 47
- Achadun Castle . . . 5B 30
- Achamore Gardens . . . 4H 15
- Achany Chambered Cairn . . . 3C 54
- Achavanich Standing Stones . . . 4E 59
- Achiltibuie Garden (summer only) . . . 3F 53
- Achnabreck Cup & Ring Marks HS . . . 4F 23
- Achnacloich Garden (summer only) . . . 5C 30
- Achness Waterfall . . . 3B 54
- Achray Forest Drive . . . 3E 25
- Achriabhach Falls . . . 2E 31
- Adam's Grave . . . 1E 17
- Aiky Brae Stone Circle . . . 2D 42
- Ailnack Gorge . . . 2E 41
- *Ailsa Craig Lighthouse* . . . 4F 9
- *Aird Laimisiadair Lighthouse, Borghastan* . . . 3F 63
- Alauna Roman Fort . . . 5D 6
- Albion Motors Museum & Archive (summer only) . . . 5F 19
- Alford Heritage Museum . . . 2A 42
- Alford Valley Railway (summer only) . . . 2A 42
- *Alford Visitor Centre* - 01975 562292 (summer only) . . . 2A 42
- Alloa Tower NTS (summer only) . . . 4H 25
- Allt na Cailliche Falls . . . 3D 38
- Almond Valley Heritage Centre . . . 2F 19
- Aluminium Story Visitor Centre . . . 2E 31
- Alva Glen . . . 4H 25
- *Alyth Museum* . . . 4H 33
- An Cala (summer only) . . . 2E 23
- An Coroghon Castle . . . 3B 36
- Ancrum Moor Battle Site 1545 . . . 1F 13
- Andrew Carnegie Birthplace Museum (summer only) . . . Dunfermline 73
- Angus's Garden . . . 1G 23
- An Iodhlann . . . 4B 28
- Annait . . . 3B 44
- Annan Museum . . . 2E 7
- Annet House Museum . . . 1E 19
- An t-Aoineadh Mor Deserted Village . . . 3H 29
- *An Tobar, Tobermory* . . . 3G 29
- *Antonine Wall (Allandale)* HS . . . 1D 18
- Antonine Wall (Callendar Park) HS . . . Falkirk 81
- Antonine Wall (Croy Hill) HS . . . 1C 18
- Antonine Wall (Dullatur, Tollpark & Garnhill) HS . . . 1C 18
- Antonine Wall (Rough Castle) HS . . . 1D 18
- *Antonine Wall (Seabegs Wood)* HS . . . 1D 18
- *Antonine Wall (Watling Lodge)* HS . . . 1D 18
- Applecross Heritage Centre (summer only) . . . 4G 45
- Arbroath Abbey (remains of) HS . . . 4D 34
- Arbroath Signal Tower Museum . . . 4D 34
- *Arbroath Visit Scotland Information Centre* - 01241 872609 . . . 4D 34
- Arbuthnot Museum . . . 4G 51
- Arbuthnott House Garden . . . 1E 35
- Ardbeg Distillery . . . 4F 15
- Ardchattan Priory Garden . . . 5C 30
- Ardchattan Priory (remains of) HS . . . 5C 30
- Ardclach Bell Tower HS . . . 4C 48
- Ardencraig Gardens (summer only) . . . 2E 17
- Ardessie Falls . . . 5F 53
- Ardestie Earth House HS . . . 5C 34
- Ardkinglas Woodland Gardens . . . 2A 24
- Ardmaddy Castle Garden . . . 2E 23
- Ardnahoe Distillery . . . 1F 15
- *Ardnamurchan Lighthouse, Kilchoan* (summer only) . . . 2F 29
- Ardnamurchan Lighthouse Visitor Centre (summer only) . . . 2F 29
- Ardnamurchan Natural History Centre (summer only) . . . 2G 29
- Ardnamurchan Point . . . 2E 29
- Ardoch Roman Fort . . . 2H 25
- *Ardrishaig Lighthouse* . . . 5F 23
- Ardrossan Castle . . . 4F 17
- *Ardrossan North Pier Lighthouse* . . . 4F 17
- Ardtornish Castle . . . 4H 29
- Ardtornish Gardens . . . 4A 30
- *Ardtreck Point Lighthouse, Carbost* . . . 5C 44
- Arduaine Garden NTS . . . 2E 23
- Ardunie Roman Signal Station HS . . . 2A 26
- Ardvreck Castle . . . 1H 53
- Ardwell Gardens (summer only) . . . 4C 4
- Argaty Red Kites . . . 3G 25
- Argyll & Sutherland Highlanders Regimental Museum . . . Stirling 87
- Argyll Forest Park . . . 4A 24
- Argyll's Lodging HS . . . Stirling 87
- Argyll Wildlife Park . . . 3H 23
- Armadale Castle Gardens (summer only) . . . 3F 37
- Arniston House (summer only) . . . 3A 20

Loch View

- Aros . . . 4D 44
- Aros Castle . . . 4G 29
- Arran Distillery . . . 4C 16
- Arthur's Seat . . . 1H 19
- Ascog Hall Victorian Fernery and Gardens (summer only) . . . 2E 17
- Assynt Visitor Centre . . . 1G 53
- Atholl Country Life Museum . . . 2D 32
- *Attadale Garden* (summer only) . . . 5A 46
- Auchagallon Stone Circle HS . . . 5B 16
- Auchentoshan Distillery . . . 1H 17
- Auchindoun Castle HS . . . 5G 49
- Auchindrain Township (summer only) . . . 3H 23
- Auchingarrich Wildlife Centre . . . 2G 25
- Auchroisk Distillery . . . 3G 49
- Auchterarder Heritage Centre . . . 2A 26
- *Auchterarder Visit Scotland Information Point* - 01764 662319 . . . 2A 26
- Auldearn Battle Site 1645 . . . 3C 48
- Auldearn Motte . . . 3C 48
- Auld Kirk Museum . . . 1B 18
- Auldton Motte . . . 3H 11
- *Aviemore Visit Scotland Information Centre* - 01479 810930 . . . Aviemore 70
- Ayr Auld Brig . . . Ayr 70
- Ayr Auld Kirk . . . Ayr 70
- *Ayr Lighthouse* . . . 1A 10
- Ayr Racecourse . . . Ayr 70
- Ayr St John's Tower . . . Ayr 70
- *Ayr Visit Scotland Information Centre* - 01292 290300 . . . Ayr 70
- *Ayton Castle (Eyemouth)* (summer only) . . . 2G 21

B

- *Baa Taing Lighthouse, Hillswick* . . . 5F 67
- Bachelors' Club NTS (summer only) . . . 1B 10
- Badbea Clearance Village . . . 2H 55
- Baird Institute . . . 2C 10
- Balbirnie Stone Circle . . . 3D 26
- Balgown Hut Circles . . . 2C 44
- *Ballachulish Tourist Information* - 01855 811866 . . . 3D 30
- *Ballachulish Visitor Centre* . . . 3D 30
- *Ballater Visit Scotland Information Centre* - 013397 55306 . . . 4G 41
- Ballindalloch Castle (summer only) . . . 5E 49
- Ballinshoe Tower . . . 3B 34
- *Balloch Visit Scotland Information Centre* - 01389 753533 (summer only) . . . 5C 24
- Balmacara Square Visitor Centre NTS . . . 1H 37
- Balmerino Abbey (remains of) NTS . . . 1E 27
- Balmoral Castle (summer only) . . . 4F 41
- Balnakeil Craft Village . . . 2E 57
- Balquhain Castle . . . 1C 42
- Balvaird Castle HS . . . 2C 26
- Balvenie Castle HS (summer only) . . . 4G 49
- Balvenie Distillery . . . 4G 49
- Balvraid Chambered Cairn . . . 2H 37
- Balwearie Castle . . . 4D 26
- Banchory Museum . . . 4B 42
- *Banchory Tourist Information Centre* - 01330 823784 . . . 4B 42
- *Banff Museum* . . . 2B 50
- *Banff Visit Scotland Information Centre* - 01261 812419 (summer only) . . . 2B 50
- Bannockburn Battle Site 1314 . . . 4G 25
- *Bannockburn Heritage Centre, Whins of Milton* NTS - 01786 812664 (summer only) . . . 4G 25
- Bargany Gardens . . . 3H 9
- Bar Hill Fort HS . . . 1C 18
- Barnes Castle . . . 1C 20
- *Barns Ness Lighthouse, Dunbar* . . . 1E 21
- Barpa Langass Chambered Cairn . . . 4J 61
- Barr Castle . . . 3G 17
- Barry Mill NTS . . . 5C 34
- Barsalloch Fort HS . . . 4E 5
- Bass of Inverurie . . . 1C 42
- Battle of Halidon Hill, The 1333 . . . 3G 21
- Battle of Homildon Hill 1402 . . . 5G 21
- Baxters Highland Village . . . 3G 49
- Bayanne House . . . 3J 67
- Bay Pottery . . . 3F 37
- Bealach na Bà . . . 4G 45
- Bearsden Bath House HS . . . 1A 18

Linlithgow

Lighthouse at Sunset

Reflection in Loch

SAFETY CAMERA INFORMATION

PocketGPSWorld.com's CamerAlert is a self-contained speed and red light camera warning system for SatNavs and Android or Apple iOS smartphones/tablets. Visit www.cameralert.com to download.

Safety camera locations are publicised by the Safer Roads Partnership which operates them in order to encourage drivers to comply with speed limits at these sites. It is the driver's absolute responsibility to be aware of and to adhere to speed limits at all times.

By showing this safety camera information it is the intention of Geographers' A-Z Map Company Ltd., to encourage safe driving and greater awareness of speed limits and vehicle speed. Data accurate at time of printing.